DEVOTIONALS FOR TWO MONTHS

NOVEMBER AND DECEMBER

Leslie M. John

DEVOTIONALS FOR TWO MONTHS

These devotionals for two months are part of series of Devotionals for a year.

The entire text of this book and graphics are deposited with Library of Congress Copyright Office, 101 Independence Avenue, SE Washington, DC 20559-6000, USA. This work is protected by Law in US; and internationally, according to The Berne Convention 1971

ISBN: 978-0-9907801-0-6

Contents

DEVOTIONALS FOR TWO MONTHS

DEVOTIONALS FOR TWO MONTHS

DEVOTIONALS FOR TWO MONTHS

PREFACE

My mission is to proclaim the good news of our Lord Jesus Christ as revealed to me through Holy Bible and from various teachers, preachers, and commentators. This is my voluntary service to God in the name of His only begotten Son Lord Jesus Christ.

I share the truth of knowledge of God with others with good intention of bringing them to the knowledge of the living God, the God of Abraham, the God of Isaac, the God of Jacob, and the Father of our Lord Jesus Christ. My mission is to proclaim the Gospel of Lord Jesus Christ and not converting forcibly anyone to Christianity.

There are fundamental Christian doctrines that I believe in and I will not compromise on those doctrines. They are:

God is Triune: The Father, The Son and The Holy Spirit. They are not three Gods, but One God in three persons, co-equal-co-existent and functionally different.

There is no salvation except by Grace through Faith in Lord Jesus Christ. I believe in:

"That if thou shalt confess with thy mouth the Lord Jesus, and shalt believe in thine heart that God hath raised him from the dead, thou shalt be saved" (Romans 10:9)

DEVOTIONALS FOR TWO MONTHS

One may accept or reject any or part of my writings/teachings. No offense is meant to any individual or any religion or any organization. Please visit http://www.lesliejohn.net/

I pray for the peace of Jerusalem and desire that all Jews may accept Lord Jesus as their personal Savior and Messiah.

"Pray for the peace of Jerusalem: they shall prosper that love thee" (Psalms 122:6)

I firmly believe in the saying of Jesus, who said:

"No man can come to me, except the Father which hath sent me draw him: and I will raise him up at the last day" John 6:44.

My efforts to teach or preach are of no use unless Lord Jesus Christ Himself intervenes and the Father draws a person unto Him.

All Scriptures in electronic format are from King James Version (KJV) from Open domain, and

English Standard Version (ESV)

Description:

God said to Joshua not to fear but meditate on the word of God day and night; "for then thou shalt make thy way prosperous".

This book of the law shall not depart out of thy mouth; but thou shalt meditate therein day and night, that thou mayest observe to do according to all that is written therein: for then thou shalt make thy way prosperous, and then thou shalt have good success. Have not I commanded thee? Be strong and of a good courage; be not afraid, neither be thou dismayed: for the LORD thy God is with thee whithersoever thou goest. (Joshua 1:8-9)

This book has 61 Devotionals to facilitate reader to meditate at least one devotional a day.

"I and my Father are one" (John 10:30)

⍰

NOVEMBER DEVOTIONALS

DAY 1 SIN BY ONE MAN'S DISOBEDIENCE

"And God is able to make all grace abound toward you; that ye, always having all sufficiency in all things, may abound to every good work" (2 Corinthians 9:8)

By one man's disobedience many were made sinners and so by the obedience of one shall be many made righteous. The righteousness does not confine to only many as few understand, but to all those who confess their sins to God and accept Jesus as their personal Savior.

The law pointed the guilt of a person but the salvation is through the grace by faith in Jesus Christ. In him alone is salvation and there is no other way for being with him for ever and ever.

Where sin abounded grace did much more abound and that is the reason why no matter how serious is the sin a man may have committed, except for blasphemy of the Holy Spirit, there is forgiveness in Jesus. Sin brought death but grace from Jesus gives us eternal life. Jesus Christ is our Lord and he is faithful to forgive us our sins.

What shall we say then, should we continue in sin that grace may abound. Apostle Paul says "God forbid". We who are dead to sin will not live in sin any longer. We are baptized into Jesus Christ into his death. (Romans 5:19-21 and Romans 6:1-3)

Those who seek to do good works and earn salvation by their own works do nullify the importance of blood of Jesus Christ. The blood of Jesus Christ that cleanses the sin has no value for them.

They diligently keep doing good works in order to receive salvation neglecting the repeated emphasis from the Lord Jesus Christ that there is eternal life only in and through him. As we read in 2 Corinthians 9:8 God is able to make grace abound to every good work. But good works are not the way for salvation. The good works follow when a man is born-again.

The blood of Jesus shed on the cross of Calvary can only save a person. This is the only way to receive eternal life. Salvation is available to all those who go to him and accept him as the Lord.

Now, here is the question :

After having been delivered from the bondage of sin by grace through faith should a child of God keep sinning because he is under the grace but not under law?

No. Never should a child of God return to sin and lose blessings from God. Salvation is not lost for those who are saved in the blood of Jesus Christ; however, the Scripture does not endorse repeated sinning. God will surely chide and chastise the one that falls repeatedly into sin and seeks grace time and again.

Should we not consider the fact that if we yield to sin we are servants to sin; and sin becomes our master? We are under grace and we should remain servants to our Lord and be obedient to put on Christ as written in Ephesians 4:24.

We were, once servants of sin; but after accepting Jesus as our master, we have become servants of righteousness. We should bear fruit unto the Lord by leading a life of holiness and have assurance that there is everlasting life for us in eternity. The law has concluded all of us under sin, but the gift of God is eternal life through Lord Jesus Christ.

"And that ye put on the new man, which after God is created in righteousness and true holiness". (Ephesians 4:24)

DAY 2 GOD QUESTIONS JOB

In day to day life we see that in every argument or quarrel there is a final say, which we call as the "last word". Likewise every dispute in the court of law has a final verdict. One wins and the other loses. There is nothing like hanging in the middle unless both the parties compromise on an issue and withdraw the case.

In the last few chapters of Job we see debate among Job, his friends, and then the final say from God. Job tried to prove himself self-righteous. Job tried to complain against God's plans. Job tried to question God. It was God who had given testimony about Job that he was upright.

"And the LORD said unto Satan, Have you considered my servant Job, that there is none like him in the earth, a blameless and an upright man, one that fears God, and turns away from evil?"(Job 1:8)

But then in due course of time when Job was found upright, he started boasting that he was righteous and justice was taken from him.

"For Job has said, I am righteous: and God has taken away my justice" (Job 34:5)

It was God's turn then to ask Job about his self-boasting and questioning God.

The questions God asked Job was to humble him and bring him to repent of his way of questioning God. It was then that God proceeds to question him in order to bring the point that Job was ignorant of several things. God shows him that he knew nothing about the foundations of the earth; nothing that limits the sea and lays boundaries to it; nothing of the clouds; nothing of the morning light; nothing about rain, frost and lightening; nothing about the secret counsels by which they are directed; nothing that directs the stars and their influence; nothing about his own soul; nothing about where the food ravens and lions get from. Job gets puzzled to listen to these questions. Some of the questions from God were…

"Where wast thou when I laid the foundations of the earth? declare, if thou hast understanding". Job 38:4

Or [who] shut up the sea with doors, when it brake forth, [as if] it had issued out of the womb?" Job 38:8

"And said, Hitherto shalt thou come, but no further: and here shall thy proud waves be stayed?" Job 38:11

"Have the gates of death been opened unto thee? or hast thou seen the doors of the shadow of death?" Job 38:17

No doubt Job suffered calamities and loss of his dear ones. No human being would, I think, can endure the hardships and sufferings Job did. Job was human too. But then, what was his strength? He depended upon God. He never ceased worshipping God. In spite of the sufferings he had to endure he never cursed God.

"Then Job answered the LORD, and said, Behold, I am vile; what shall I answer thee? I will lay mine hand upon my mouth. Once have I spoken; but I will not answer: yea, twice; but I will proceed no further." Job 40:3-6

Brother/Sister,

Let us introspect if we are questioning God's wisdom or plans. Let us remember that His thoughts are higher than ours. He is our maker and we are the people of His pasture. He is the potter and we are the vessels.

Isaiah 55:9 reads, "For [as] the heavens are higher than the earth, so are my ways higher than your ways, and my thoughts than your thoughts."

Romans 9:21 reads, "Hath not the potter power over the clay, of the same lump to make one vessel unto honour, and another unto dishonour?"

Jesus my Savior I worship You
Jesus my Lord I praise You,
Jesus my God I thank You
Jesus the Son of God I adore You.

DAY 3 ISRAEL

God named Jacob as Israel and loved Israel more than we can imagine. He has called Israel as His first born son.

It is not a name given by human but it is the name that is given by God; it is "Israel", which in Hebrew means God has striven, or God has saved. "And he said, Thy name shall be called no more Jacob, but Israel: for as a prince hast thou power with God and with men, and hast prevailed." Genesis 32:28. The descendants of Jacob are Israel. To be specific, the tribe of Judah, and the tribe of Benjamin, and those, who are from the tribe of Levi, who have joined with Judah are called, 'Jews'; and the rest of them are called, "Israel". God has given great privilege to the "Israel" as a whole to be called as His first born. "And thou shalt say unto Pharaoh, Thus saith the LORD, Israel is my son, even my firstborn" Exodus 4:22

A woman stricken with devil approached Jesus for healing of her daughter, crying "O Lord, thou Son of David; my daughter is grievously vexed with a devil" but Jesus replied, " ... I am not sent but unto the lost sheep of the house of Israel." Matthew 15:24. However, because of her faith in acknowledging her lowliness, when she said to Jesus, " yet the dogs eat of the crumbs which fall from their masters' table", "Then Jesus answered and said unto her, O woman, great is thy faith: be it unto thee even as thou wilt. And her daughter was made whole from that very hour". The woman was gentile; her plea was heard by Jesus because He had compassion on her. This is a mystery not seen in the Old Testament.

God blessed Abraham and said, whoever blesses Abraham will be blessed and whoever curses Abraham will be cursed, and likewise, God gave the privilege to Israel only to be called as Israel.

Whoever calls himself/herself a 'Jew' or 'Israel', and not a Jew or Israel will face the anger of the Lord. "I know thy works, and tribulation, and poverty, (but thou art rich) and I know the blasphemy of them which say they are Jews, and are not, but are the synagogue of Satan". Revelation 2:9.

It is very serious to identify oneself as "Jew" when one is not a Jew. Jacob and his descendants had all the priority in the presence of the Lord. "The portion of Jacob is not like them: for he is the former of all things; and Israel is the rod of his inheritance: The LORD of hosts is his name". Jeremiah 10:16

Yet, when it comes to the Church, the Church is His bride, heavenly possession. The Church stands over the Israel and the Jews. God fulfilled most of the covenants made to the children of Israel. The restoration of the kingdom unto them is yet to come.

Jesus will reign from the throne of David for one thousand years after restoration of the kingdom to them. Unto this end the 'great tribulation' lasts and unto this end the delay occurs in the coming of Jesus again. Do not believe false prophets, false preachers, who predict the day of coming of Jesus. The Church will be 'caught up' when Jesus comes again.

For the Lord himself shall descend from heaven with a shout, with the voice of the archangel, and with the trump of God: and the dead in Christ shall rise first: Then we which are alive and remain shall be caught up together with them in the clouds, to meet the Lord in the air: and so shall we ever be with the Lord. (1 Thessalonians 4:16-17)

DAY 4 ABRAHAM FEARED

We see in the following exposition that Abram, whose name God changed as "Abraham" feared and attempted to escape from trouble. Before we go into meditating on this thought let us recollect a verse from New Testament.

2 Timothy 3:16 reads...

"All scripture is given by inspiration of God, and is profitable for doctrine, for reproof, for correction, for instruction in righteousness..."

Now, here is the message from Genesis Chapter 20

After living for twenty years in Mamre Abram sojourned to Gerar. Abram was also called sojourner. He moved from one place to another. We are also sojourners on this earth looking forward to reaching heaven, which is our final destination. When Abram moved from Mamre to Gerar, he was afraid for some time and tried to lie. That appears to us as unbecoming of his stature as the father of faith. It also renders him the character of cowardice.

At a time when Sarai, whose name God changed later as "Sarah", was with a child, a promised seed in her womb, he asked her to say that she was his sister. He was worried more about his own life than living up to the truth.

Abram's own words say: "And yet indeed she is my sister; she is the daughter of my father, but not the daughter of my mother; and she became my wife. (Genesis 20:12)"

Yet, since he married her she was his wife. In his attempt to escape from trouble he said to her that she may tell Abimelech that she was his sister. Because of the fear Abram had Abimelech, the king of Gerar excels in character. The one who was about to commit sin is restored.

Abimelech sent for Sarai, and took her to his house with a sinful desire to the take her to his bed. Note that usually one sin paves the way for another.

It is indeed disastrous, especially when the sin of God's child paves the way for ungodly to commit sin. Let us, as the children of God, examine ourselves, if our ways are leading others to commit sins.

Because God made covenant with Abram He intervened and prevented the ugliest situation to come up. Psalmist asserts in Psalm 105:13-15 "When they went from one nation to another, from one kingdom to another people; He suffered no man to do them wrong: yea, he reproved kings for their sakes; saying, touch not mine anointed, and do my prophets no harm.

"And the LORD plagued Pharaoh and his house with great plagues because of Sarai Abram's wife" (Genesis 12:17)

God appeared to Abimelech, King of Gerar, in a dream and gave him warning that he was going to commit sin. God revealed to

Abimelech that Sarai was Abram's wife. He also gets warning that if he forces her into illegal relationship he will face death.

Abimelech pleads innocent before God and implores for mercy. He prays that he and his nation may not be punished. God grants Abimelech his petition and imputes him no sin.

One aspect that needs to be noted here is that a great deal of sin was devised but it was not executed. More often than not, God restrains people to commit sin.

No temptation is beyond the control of men, and in fact in every situation God provides a way out. It is by our willful act that we fall in to sin, or lead others into sin. In situations where we choose to fall willfully into sin against the will of God we are responsible and accountable. Let us be careful.

"There hath no temptation taken you but such as is common to man: but God is faithful, who will not suffer you to be tempted above that ye are able; but will with the temptation also make a way to escape, that ye may be able to bear it" (1 Corinthians 10:13)

DAY 5 GOD'S LOVE

"Behold, what manner of love the Father hath bestowed upon us, that we should be called the sons of God: therefore the world knoweth us not, because it knew him not" (1 John 3:1)

It is the abundant love that God bestowed upon us that we are called and made sons of God and upon seeing Jesus we shall be like him as he is.

The world does not know this mystery, nor would it understand the love that God has bestowed upon us to make sons of God. The reason is simple; it is because the world does not know the God of gods, and the Lord of lords, and the King of kings, who loved us and sent his one and only begotten Son that whosoever believes in him shall not perish but have everlasting life.

There is a responsibility given to the children of God, who loved us, and demands from us that we should lead a pure life even as he is pure.

It is not that we are infallible, and our salvation will be lost if we commit sins, inadvertently, or deliberately, but the Word of God says that he who commits sins is of the devil, because devil sinned from the beginning, and keeps tempting the children of God, to fall into sins.

Whosoever sins transgresses the law, and the transgression of the law is Sin. Whosoever abides in the Lord, and born-again does not sin, and whoever sins has not understood His love.

Apostle John exhorts that let no man deceive us about righteousness, but understand clearly that he who does righteousness is righteous, even as the Lord is righteous.

It is not because of our good works or ability to save ourselves that we are saved, but because Jesus paid price for our salvation that we are saved and his righteousness is imputed to us.

There was a man of the Pharisees, named Nicodemus, a ruler of the Jews:

The same came to Jesus by night, and said unto him, Rabbi, we know that you are a teacher come from God: for no man can do these miracles that you do, except God be with him.

Jesus answered and said unto him, Verily, verily, I say unto you, Except a man be born again, he cannot see the kingdom of God.

Nicodemus said unto him, How can a man be born when he is old? can he enter the second time into his mother's womb, and be born?

Jesus answered, Verily, verily, I say unto you, Except a man be born of water and of the Spirit, he cannot enter into the kingdom of God.

That which is born of the flesh is flesh; and that which is born of the Spirit is spirit. (John 3:1-6)

DAY 6 SEEK HEAVENLY THINGS

Many times when people think that their lives are best fortified the life quickly and easily ends and they leave behind their assets for someone else, not even their close ones, to enjoy. King Solomon enjoyed every kind of blessing and was happy.

He acknowledges that God loves a man who is good before Him. He says all the days of a greedy man trying to earn more and more in his life are filled with sorrow, travail and grief with no rest in the night.

He says God gives a man who is good in his sight wisdom, knowledge and joy, but to the sinner he gives travail, to gather up and to heap up more. He says it is vanity and vexation of spirit. (Ecclesiastes 2:22-26)

Jesus questions how does it profit man who gains the whole world and loses his own soul? What could a man give in exchange for his soul? To be rich is not sin but fraudulent gain and cheating is sin.

Trying to gain riches at the cost of working for God does no good. Matthew 16:26-28 say that Jesus will reward every man according to his works. Apostle Paul also says in 2 Corinthians 5:10 that we shall all stand before the judgment seat of Christ to receive rewards for working for Jesus.

It is indeed hard for a child of God to be in the world and be out of the temptations that this world brings into the lives of a believer.

The life in this world for a believer in Christ is not a bed of roses. Satan is always at work. "And no marvel; for Satan himself is transformed into an angel of light". (2 Corinthians 11:14) Unless a believer takes refuge in Christ and encounters Satan in the name of Jesus not even the best and strong believer would win over Satan.

Believer has constant struggle against the desires of possession of wealth and not falling into lusts of this world. The wise king Solomon drifted from his good path and married many wives and had concubines.

More than his sin of being polygamist having married seven hundred wives, princesses and three hundred concubines he went after other gods namely Ashteroth, the Milcom (1 Kings 11:3 -5). God promised that Solomon's throne will be established for ever and ever but He would chastise Solomon for his iniquity. (2 Samuel 7:13-14)

It so often bothers the mind of believer as how to clothe himself, how will he have food to eat and how will his needs be met with. Jesus asked to take a note of how the lilies of the field grow.

He said they neither spin nor do they toil yet Solomon in all his glory was not arrayed like one of them. Jesus asked to have faith that if God can clothe the grass of the field he shall clothe us too (Matthew 6:28-30)

It is, therefore, wise to do some works to gather for ourselves treasures in heaven where neither moth nor rust corrupts our wealth instead of storing up for ourselves treasures upon this earth where moth and rust corrupts and where thieves break through and steal. (Matthew 6:19-20)

Apostle Paul says if we are risen with Christ we should seek the things which are above where Christ sits on the right hand of God and not set our affection on the things on this earth.

"If ye then be risen with Christ, seek those things which are above, where Christ sitteth on the right hand of God. Set your affection on things above, not on things on the earth" (Colossians 3:1-2)

DAY 7 AHAZIAH

GOD'S ANGER OVER WORSHIPPING IDOLS

This devotional is from II Kings Chapter 1

Ahaziah was son of Ahab. "Ahaziah the son of Ahab began to reign over Israel in Samaria the seventeenth year of Jehoshaphat king of Judah, and reigned two years over Israel". (1 Kings 22:51)

This is about the king Ahaziah, who fell down from his upper chamber through the lattice and became sick. The king sent his messengers to Baalzebub, the god of Ekron to know if he would have recovery from the disease. (Baalzebub was believed to be a god of Philistines.

He was believed to have given out oracles and protected them from flies, and therefore, he was also known as "the Lord of flies" [Ref. International Standard Bible Encyclopedia and Geneva Bible footnotes]). Ekron was one of the cities in the northern part of Israel. (Ref: Joshua 15:11; 1Samuel 5:10; 6:16-17).

Ahaziah hoped in a god made in the form of idol by man. He purposed to know if he would have recovery from the injuries and the disease that he suffered after his fall through the lattice from his upper chamber.

As if the God of Israel, who redeemed them from the bondage of slavery under Pharaoh, was not strong enough, Ahaziah depended on some material that appeared like god.

God was very angry over Ahaziah's reliance on Baalzebub, an idol god at Ekron. The Angel of the Lord said to Elijah the Tishbite, to ask Ahaziah if his dependency on idol was because he thought there was no living God in Israel. Elijah met the messengers from Ahaziah on their way to Ekron, and said the words that the Angel of the Lord had put in his mouth.

"Now therefore thus saith the LORD, Thou shalt not come down from that bed on which thou art gone up, but shalt surely die. And Elijah departed" (2 Kings 1:4)

The messengers returned to Ahaziah and Ahaziah asked them how the man who spoke those words looked like. The messengers described him as a man in a hairy garment, and girt with a girdle of leather. Ahaziah recognized that he was Elijah the Tishbite, who spoke those words and he sent to him a captain of fifty with his fifty. The captain of fifty with his fifty said to Elijah the Tishbite to go with them to the king.

"And Elijah answered and said to the captain of fifty, If I be a man of God, then let fire come down from heaven, and consume thee and thy fifty. And there came down fire from heaven, and consumed him and his fifty". (2 Kings 1:10)

Ahaziah sent another captain of fifty with his fifty. The captain said to Elijah to go to the king quickly.

"And Elijah answered and said unto them, If I be a man of God, let fire come down from heaven, and consume thee and thy fifty. And the fire of God came down from heaven, and consumed him and his fifty" (2 Kings 1:12)

Then, Ahaziah's third captain of fifty went to Elijah and fell on his knees before him and begged him to spare his life and the lives of his fifty men.

Fire came down from heaven and consumed the two former captains and their fifty men each, but this time, the Angel of the Lord said to Elijah not to be afraid but go with him. Elijah obeyed the word from the Angel of the Lord and stood before the king and asked him if it was because he thought that there was no living God in Israel that he sent his messengers to Baalzebub, the god of Ekron.

Elijah said to Ahaziah that because he believed and relied on the god made by man for his healing, instead of depending on the living God, he would not rise from his bed but die.

According to the word of Jehovah that Elijah spoke to Ahaziah, the king Ahaziah died and his place was taken by Jehoram, the son of Jehoshaphat, king of Judah. (Ahaziah had no son).

Let us hope in the Living God, for all our needs, may they be sickness or any other need.

"For we are saved by hope: but hope that is seen is not hope: for what a man seeth, why doth he yet hope for? But if we hope

for that we see not, then do we with patience wait for it".
(Romans 8:24-25)

DAY 8 APOSTASY

2 Thessalonians 2:2-3 "That ye be not soon shaken in mind, or be troubled, neither by spirit, nor by word, nor by letter as from us, as that the day of Christ is at hand. Let no man deceive you by any means: for that day shall not come, except there come a falling away first, and that man of sin be revealed, the son of perdition"

In 2 Thess.2:3 there is a reference to 'falling away'. This word 'falling away' means that there will be apostasy. It also means that there will be deviation from the truth. It will be the beginning of sorrows when Antichrist is revealed.

Those who hate Jesus will hand over believers to persecutions (Matt 24:9 and 10). The yielding to such persecutions will come as a result of the aggressive demands from the false teachers, temptations, and worldliness.

Those, who do not have enough knowledge of Jesus Christ, would yield to such persecutions, and those, who are strong enough in faith will resist such temptations, and persecutions.

These persecutions are the result of 'great tribulation' from Antichrist, the 'man of sin', who is also called the 'son of perdition'. Antichrist will be revealed to the world, when Holy Spirit, the restrainer, who comforts believers in Christ, ceases to work in the world. The revealing of Antichrist will not be until the Holy Spirit, the 'restrainer' is taken away from the way.

The believers, who are living and waiting for the Lord Jesus Christ to come again, will be 'caught up' together with those, who are dead in Christ. The dead in Christ will rise first to meet the Lord in the air and we, who are living and remain, shall be 'caught up' together with them in the clouds to be with the Lord for ever.

There is no reason for the believers in Christ to be sorrowful or worried about the things that shall come to pass after they are 'caught up'.

It shall be the time for we, the believers to receive rewards at the 'Bema seat', while we are with the Lord in the clouds, as referred to in 2 Corinthians 5:10 and 1Peter 5:4 for the works that we have done on this earth.

True, we do not want to gain the whole world and lose our soul. Our works should be to gain rewards from our Lord at the 'Bema Seat', when we are with the Lord Jesus Christ, on His coming in the clouds.

During the 'great tribulation' period Israel will cry for the Lord's mercy. This period is also called, "Jacob's Trouble" "Alas! for that day is great, so that none is like it: it is even the time of Jacob's trouble; but he shall be saved out of it". (Jeremiah 30:7)

Romans 11:28-32 "As concerning the gospel, they are enemies for your sakes: but as touching the election, they are beloved for the fathers' sakes.

For the gifts and calling of God are without repentance. For as ye in times past have not believed God, yet have now obtained mercy through their unbelief: Even so have these also now not believed, that through your mercy they also may obtain mercy. For God hath concluded them all in unbelief, that he might have mercy upon all".

DAY 9 BEHOLD THY SON

One of the seven sayings of Jesus on the cross was:

"Behold thy son"... and he continued saying ... "Behold thy mother"

When Jesus therefore saw his mother, and the disciple standing by, whom he loved, he saith unto his mother, Woman, behold thy son! Then saith he to the disciple, Behold thy mother! And from that hour that disciple took her unto his own home. (John 19:26-27)

When Jesus was in human form having relinquished his glory to become one like us He honored his mother. When he was hung on the cross he gave the responsibility, to one of his disciples John, to look after his mother.

Likewise Jesus also comforted his mother that his disciple John, whom he loved, would be her son from then onwards. Jesus showed great love towards everybody on this earth. His love included healing, forgiving sins, and bearing our sins upon himself.

Jesus was the Son of God, who had divine nature in himself while on this earth, in addition to having human nature. He replied to his mother, once, that he came into this world to do His Father's business.

The Father's business in him and through him was to glorify the Father's name and accept crucifixion bearing our sins upon him in order to redeem us from the bondage of sin.

His Father's business was more important for him, but he did not neglect his responsibilities while he was on this earth. Mary the earthly mother of Jesus and Joseph did not find him after their one day's journey while returning from Jerusalem to their native place Galilee. They had been to Jerusalem to celebrate Passover feast.

They supposed that Jesus, who was then a twelve-year old boy, was in their company but having not found him in their company they returned to Jerusalem and found him sitting in the temple learning in the midst of doctors, hearing and asking them questions.

They did not find him until three days past and when they found him they were surprised to see that all who heard him were astonished at his understanding and answers. They were all amazed.

At this time Mary, as a human, and concern for him, asked Jesus why he dealt with them in that way and said she and Joseph were seeking for him with sorrow. (Luke 2:44-48) It is at that time that Jesus replied to her saying, "And he said unto them, How is it that ye sought me? wist ye not that I must be about my Father's business?" (Luke 2:49)

However, when he was breathing his last on the cross having taken up on himself our sins, he said to his mother, "Behold thy son" and to his disciple John, whom he loved he said "Behold thy mother"

Jesus fulfilled every responsibility that was given to him upon this earth before he died for our sake. He was buried and rose on the third day. Later, he ascended into heaven and seated on the right hand of the Majesty. He promised that all those who have accepted him as their savior will have everlasting life and be with him for ever and ever.

DAY 10 DARKNESS IN DAY TIME

Eli, Eli, lama sabachthani?
(My God, my God, why hast thou forsaken me?)

From Matthew 27:46

"Now from the sixth hour there was darkness over all the land unto the ninth hour. And about the ninth hour Jesus cried with a loud voice, saying, Eli, Eli, lama sabachthani? that is to say, My God, my God, why hast thou forsaken me?" (Matthew 27:45-46)

From the sixth hour of the day in Jerusalem until the ninth of hour there, which is equivalent to 12.00 PM to 3.00 PM of our time, there was utter darkness on the face of the earth when Jesus was on the cross, bearing our sin upon Himself.

It pleased the Father to bruise His Son Jesus for our sin (cf. prophecy in Isaiah 53:10), and our sin was judged at the cross by the righteous Lord God.

"Yet it pleased the LORD to bruise him; he hath put him to grief: when thou shalt make his soul an offering for sin, he shall see his seed, he shall prolong his days, and the pleasure of the LORD shall prosper in his hand" (Isaiah 53:10)

It was at that time that the Father brought about severest darkness on the face of the earth. Jesus took our punishment on Himself and our sin on Him was judged at the Cross. The Father, the Holy One, could not see the sin on the Son Jesus Christ, and that is the reason why the Father judged the sin at the cross where Lord Jesus was hung bearing our sin. Darkness signifies judgment and during this darkness our sin was judged at the Cross.

"For he hath made him to be sin for us, who knew no sin; that we might be made the righteousness of God in him" (2 Corinthians 5:21)

"Christ hath redeemed us from the curse of the law, being made a curse for us: for it is written, Cursed is every one that hangeth on a tree" (Galatians 3:13)

"his body shall not remain all night on the tree, but you shall bury him the same day, for a hanged man is cursed by God. You shall not defile your land that the LORD your God is giving you for an inheritance" (Deuteronomy 21:23 ESV)

Jesus, who knew no sin, was made sin for us in order that we might be made the righteousness of God in Him. There are contentious beliefs that Father can look upon the sin of man, and therefore, Jesus was not forsaken; but considering the fact that sin is pernicious, heinous, offensive and polluted, it is hardly believable that the Holy Father God could see sin upon the Son of God.

In the Old Testament according to the Law, Moses was commanded by the LORD, to burn the bullock, and his hide, his flesh and his dung outside the camp. This shadow was fulfilled in Jesus when the sin on Him was judged at Golgotha, outside the city, in order that He may become propitiation and die a substitutionary death on behalf of us to redeem us to give us everlasting life. Anyone can receive this everlasting life by believing that Jesus is the Lord and God raised Him from the dead.

"But the bullock, and his hide, his flesh, and his dung, he burnt with fire without the camp; as the LORD commanded Moses" (Leviticus 8:17)

It was neither an eclipse nor was the usual darkness that came at sunset, but it was utter darkness from noon to three past noon. It was during the Passover that this darkness came upon the face of the earth and this darkness prevailed on the face of the earth in the midst of the day light. It was indeed unusual.

"Verily, verily, I say unto you, He that heareth my word, and believeth on him that sent me, hath everlasting life, and shall not come into condemnation; but is passed from death unto life". (John 5:24)

Darkness was one of the ten plagues that God brought on Egypt. "And the LORD said unto Moses, Stretch out thine hand toward heaven, that there may be darkness over the land of Egypt, even darkness [which] may be felt. And Moses stretched forth his hand toward heaven; and there was a thick darkness in all the land of Egypt three days" Exodus 10:21,22

"And it came between the camp of the Egyptians and the camp of Israel; and it was a cloud and darkness to them, but it gave light by night to these: so that the one came not near the other all the night". (Exodus 14:20)

Darkness is accompanied with fear, sin, and judgment. It is opposed to luster and honor. It is opposed to wisdom; it is associated with confusion, folly, vexation of Spirit, and calamities. An angel shone light towards Israelites when Israelites were just about to cross Red Sea, and darkness to Pharaoh and his army. It was the judgment that Pharaoh and his army were about to face while the children of God were about to cross the Red Sea.

Scriptures speak of the sun and the moon getting fully darkened, and the stars withdrawing their shining in the last days. It happens when the Lord comes again to this earth.

"The sun and the moon shall be darkened, and the stars shall withdraw their shining". (Joel 3:15)

When Jesus was on the cross he quoted directly from Psalm 22:1 and cried aloud "Eli, Eli, lama sabachthani? that is to say, My God, my God, why hast thou forsaken me?"

"My God, my God, why hast thou forsaken me? why art thou so far from helping me, and from the words of my roaring?" (Psalms 22:1)

Although the details of separation or non-separation of the Father and the Son at the cross, for a while, are known to the Father and the Son only, yet it is worth considering, to the best of our knowledge, whether or not the Son was forsaken at the Lord's death and why Lord Jesus said "My God, my God, why hast thou forsaken me?" It is necessary that we understand what exactly happened during those dark hours, and the way the Father judged sin upon the Son.

Lord Jesus had two natures in His incarnation when He relinquished His glory that He had with the Father and came into this world in the form of a servant and in the likeness of man. One nature that He had was of divine and the other of human. He felt the human traits such as joy, pain, sadness, hunger. He wept at the tomb of Lazarus, who was dead for four days. However, the pain He suffered at the cross was, indeed, much more in its intensity. He bore our sin and took the penalty of our sin upon Himself and paid for our sin and punishment. It was not by silver or by gold that we were redeemed but by His precious blood, and therefore, the cost of our redemption was very heavy.

Lord Jesus felt separation from the Father just as the David felt separation from God but the Lord was not forsaken to be our savior or ceased to be God. He was for a short while, in His human nature, felt all alone while our sin was on Him. God is Almighty, who is triune, and who lives forever and ever, is inseparable. God is omnipresent, omniscient, and omnipotent.

"Thus saith the LORD, The heaven is my throne, and the earth is my footstool: where is the house that ye build unto me? and where is the place of my rest?" (Isaiah 66:1)

It would also be apt to consider here whether or not David felt separation from God when He cried "My God, my God, why hast thou forsaken me? why art thou so far from helping me, and from the words of my roaring?" (Psalms 22:1)

The caption of the Psalm is "To the chief Musician upon Aijeleth Shahar, A Psalm of David" David was singing a song extemporarily, an unknown tune, pointing to Lord Jesus Christ's sufferings than to himself. It was an unknown future to him. When He sang the song He neither felt Jesus would be separated from the Father or not but He said "My God, my God why hast thou forsaken me" in prophecy. The psalm is Messianic. He did not mean Jesus would be separated or would not be separated; however the word meaning of "forsaken" is abandon.

David lost fellowship with God when He had illegal relationship with Bathsheba and got her husband Uriah killed. His sin did not go unpunished. God dealt with Him severely but taking away his firstborn son, and putting him to terrible ignominy (Ref. 2 Samuel 12:1-19).

Similarly when Jesus was on the cross He, in His human nature was bearing our sin and that sin was judged severely by the Father and Jesus felt separation from the Father; however God raised Him from the dead and said to Him "You are my Son, today I have begotten you".

So also Christ did not exalt himself to be made a high priest, but was appointed by him who said to him, "You are my Son, today I have begotten you"; (Hebrews 5:5 ESV)

Psalmist goes on singing the song indicating the Lord's exaltation in His future kingdom. He concludes the psalm in praises and the Lord's exaltation as the King.

"All the prosperous of the earth eat and worship; before him shall bow all who go down to the dust, even the one who could not keep himself alive. Posterity shall serve him; it shall be told of the Lord to the coming generation; they shall come and proclaim his righteousness to a people yet unborn, that he has done it" (Psalm 22:29-31 ESV)

Lord Jesus said:

"I and my Father are one". (John 10:30)

Although the word "forsaken" in Hebrew, Greek and in English means "abandon" Lord Jesus Christ was not forsaken eternally, but He felt separation from the Father, because He was bearing our sin upon Himself, and that is why He was quoting from Psalm 22:1 when He cried "My God, my God, why hast thou forsaken me?"

"And about the ninth hour Jesus cried with a loud voice, saying, Eli, Eli, lama sabachthani? that is to say, My God, my God, why hast thou forsaken me?" (Matthew 27:46)

Let us worship the Father in the name of our Lord and Savior Jesus Christ, who was crucified, died for our sake, was buried and was raised from the dead on the third day. Jesus ascended into heaven and he is seated on the right hand of the Majesty.

DAY 11 DAVID HONORED GOD

David depended upon God before waging wars. Before he went for war against Philistines he enquired of the Lord saying "Shall I go up to the Philistines?" and God asked him to go ahead.

"And David enquired of the LORD, saying, Shall I go up to the Philistines? wilt thou deliver them into mine hand? And the LORD said unto David, Go up: for I will doubtless deliver the Philistines into thine hand" (2 Samuel 5:19)

David not only put an end to Philistines who troubled the children of Israel but he also defeated Moabites. He also defeated Hadadezer, the son of Rehob, king of Zobab and recovered his border at the river Euphrates.

David smote Syrians and they became servants to David and brought gifts. Edomites also became servants of David and the Almighty God preserved David wherever he went. (2 Samuel 8:14)

David dedicated unto God the silver and gold that he had from all nations which he subdued. David's administration and organization was excellent. David administered judgment and justice to all people. (2 Samuel 8:11,15 and 18)

"And David reigned over all Israel; and David executed judgment and justice unto all his people" (2 Samuel 8:15)

King David's sincere worship of God is seen in many references. He thought of building a temple for God but God allowed his son Solomon to build the temple at Jerusalem.

Speaking to Solomon David said that it was in his mind to build a house unto the name of God, but God said to him that David had shed blood abundantly upon the earth in His sight, and made great wars, and, therefore, he should not build a house unto His name.

God said that his son Solomon would build a house unto the name of the Lord. God promised that He would establish Solomon's throne for ever over Israel. He wished that God may give wisdom and understanding to Solomon to keep the law of the Lord.

David assured Solomon that if he kept the law of the Lord, he would prosper. He encouraged his son to be of good courage, not to dread, or dismayed. David helped him and said:

"Now, behold, in my trouble I have prepared for the house of the LORD an hundred thousand talents of gold, and a thousand thousand talents of silver; and of brass and iron without weight; for it is in abundance: timber also and stone have I prepared; and thou mayest add thereto" (1 Chronicles 22:14)

God honors who honor him. God blessed David and Solomon abundantly.

"And when he had removed him, he raised up unto them David to be their king; to whom also he gave testimony, and said, I have found David the son of Jesse, a man after mine own heart, which shall fulfil all my will". (Acts 13:22)

DAY 12 DAVID REPENTS

David was a man of wars and God was with him. However, on one occasion when David yielded to Satan's temptation and numbered Israel he had to seek atonement for his sin.

Satan had David yield to his temptation and stand in his pride to number Israel and look upon his own strength. All the days of his life God helped him win the wars with small number in his army.

If we recall David's victory over Goliath it can be seen that he brought down the proud and hefty Philistine with just one smooth stone out of the five that he has collected from the brook. He put the five stones in a shepherd's bag that he had and swung his sling with just one stone in it and brought down the Philistine onto the ground. Then, David ran and stood upon Goliath and drew the sword from Goliath's sheath and killed him. (1 Samuel 17:40 and 51)

Lord Jesus Christ said "But when a stronger than he shall come upon him, and overcome him, he taketh from him all his armour wherein he trusted, and divideth his spoils". (Luke 11:22)

"And Satan stood up against Israel, and provoked David to number Israel" (1 Chronicles 21:1)

In spite of Joab's efforts to try to prevent David to trespass against God's desires and against Israel, David's orders prevailed and Joab numbered the Israel. God was angry at David and his actions in numbering Israel.

God sent an angel to destroy Jerusalem and as the angel of the LORD was destroying Jerusalem, David repented of the evil he did and said to the angel to stop destroying. He saw the angel of the Lord standing between the earth and heaven having a drawn sword in his hand stretched out over Jerusalem. David and elders of Israel wore sack clothes and fell upon their faces.

David accepted that he sinned against God and prayed that he may be punished but not his people because it was he who sinned against the Lord. The LORD saw that David repented of his sin.

David built an altar in the threshing floor of Ornan the Jebusite, according to the desire of the LORD as ordered by the angel of the LORD through Gad who conveyed the words of the angel of the LORD to him.

David paid full price of the land, the oxen, and the threshing instruments for wood and also for wheat that was needed for the meat offering.

 David refused to take all these free of cost. He paid Ornan, six hundred shekels of gold by weight. David built there an altar unto the LORD. The LORD, then asked the angel of the LORD to put his sword in his sheath. When David saw that the LORD answered his prayer in the threshing floor of Ornan, he sacrificed there. (1 Chronicles 21:28)

There is reconciliation when we pray and accept before God our sins. God forgives us our iniquity.

DAY 13 DAVID'S THRONE

David's throne established for ever

Houses made of wooden were considered as posh living Houses in the Old Testament period, more so, if they were made of Cedar wood. King David was living in such a house made of Cedar wood (2 Samuel 5:11).

One day David expressed his concern to Nathan the prophet that while he himself was living in a house made of Cedar wood the Ark of God was within the curtains (2 Samuel 7:2).

King David had an intention to build a house for God. The prophet, although he was from God, spoke this time instantaneously without seeking counsel from God and said that the King may do what was in his mind. However, God spoke to Nathan the prophet and asked him to go and question David, if he is capable of building a house for God to dwell in!

God spoke to David through Nathan the prophet that all along when the children of Israel journeyed from Egypt to Canaan God did not have any place to dwell in except for a tent and a tabernacle. God questioned if He asked at any time from any of the tribes of Israel any favor to build a Cedar house for himself. God reminded David that He gave all the instructions and commandments from a tent and from tabernacle. God asked David to recollect his own position from where he was made to rise. David was a mere shepherd and yet God made him ruler over the children of Israel and not only God was with him but

God made his name to be greater than any king upon this earth. All his enemies were cut out of his sight and his name was made great like that of great men who were on the earth.

God said that he will appoint a place for his people Israel and plant them that they would dwell in a place of their own. God assured that He would not allow wicked people to afflict the children of Israel any more as they did before.

After bringing the children of Israel from out of Egypt into Canaan God commanded judges to be over his people Israel and later David was made the King. God caused David to rest from all his enemies.

God told David that He will make a house for David and when his days are fulfilled he will sleep with his fathers. God promised to set up David's seed and establish his kingdom for ever. God indicated that King Solomon will build a house for God's name and establish his throne of his kingdom for ever.

God said that if Solomon committed any iniquity he would chastise him with rod of men, and with the stripes of the children of men, but His mercy will not depart from him.

King David humbled himself after hearing God's word through Nathan the prophet and exalted the name of God by saying:

"Wherefore thou art great, O LORD God: for there is none like thee, neither is there any God beside thee, according to all that we have heard with our ears" (2 Samuel 7:22)

"And let thy name be magnified for ever, saying, The LORD of hosts is the God over Israel: and let the house of thy servant David be established before thee" (2 Samuel 7:26)

DAY 14 DEAD IN CHRIST

"For the Lord himself shall descend from heaven with a shout, with the voice of the archangel, and with the trump of God: and the dead in Christ shall rise first: Then we which are alive and remain shall be caught up together with them in the clouds, to meet the Lord in the air: and so shall we ever be with the Lord" (1 Thessalonians 4:16-17)

'The dead in Christ shall rise first and the living saints shall be caught up together with them in the clouds to meet the Lord in the air'. This blessed hope is given to us that we will be with the Lord for ever.

The resurrection of the dead with the glorified bodies will be 'in a moment, in the twinkling of an eye at the last trump: for the trumpet shall sound, and the dead shall be raised incorruptible, and we shall be changed' before the commencement of Daniel's Seventieth week, that is 'great tribulation'.

"But every man in his own order: Christ the first-fruits; afterward they that are Christ's at his coming" 1 Corinthians 15:23. There are several reasons to believe that the 'rapture' precedes the 'great tribulation' and that believers in Christ will not see or be part of the 'great tribulation'. Jesus Christ's second coming will be personal and visible. The Lord will descend from heaven with a shout, with the voice of the archangel and with the 'trump of God'.

The Church (Ekklesia) is the precious possession of Lord Jesus Christ and, therefore, it is His love for the Church, and the faithfulness that He has toward His bride that He keeps His bride away from the earthly 'great tribulation', which is primarily for the earthly people and for those, who have rejected Lord Jesus Christ as their Messiah.

Those, who have accepted Jesus as their personal Savior and Lord, by confessing their sins to Him are the treasured possession of Him, and He protects them from the 'great tribulation, which is meant for the children of Israel, who have rejected as their Messiah.

Two fold purposes of Lord Jesus Christ coming to this earth, is to restore the children of Israel their earthly kingdom, which God had promised to their fathers, and also for the heathen to see God's judgment on those, who sinned and rejected Him as their Savior.

The Church always remains with Him with heavenly blessings showered on them by God and are away from the earthly things. That is the reason why when Lord Jesus Christ descends from heaven in the clouds with a shout, with the voice of archangel, those saints, who are dead in Christ shall rise first and those, who are alive and remain shall be caught up together with them in the clouds, to meet Him in the air, and thereafter we will be with Him for ever.

"It is sown a natural body; it is raised a spiritual body. There is a natural body, and there is a spiritual body". (1 Corinthians 15:44)

"In a moment, in the twinkling of an eye, at the last trump: for the trumpet shall sound, and the dead shall be raised incorruptible, and we shall be changed". (1 Corinthians 15:52)"

DAY 15 SENNACHERIB

Be strong and courageous, be not afraid nor dismayed by the king of Assyria, nor by all the multitude that is with him: for there are more with us than with him: (2 Chronicles 32:7)

There was a King by name, Sennacherib. He was known for his pride, blasphemous nature, and ridiculing attitude. 2 Chronicles Chapter 32 has the details of Sennacherib's downfall and Hezekiah's victory.

Sennacherib sent blasphemous letters to Hezekiah, ridiculing the God of Hezekiah. Sennacherib had ambition of besieging Lachish (v. 9), but hears that Hezekiah is fortifying Jerusalem and encouraging his people to stand against the invasion.

Sennacherib comes in person to besiege it and before he wages a war against Jerusalem, he sends messengers to make speeches demeaning the living God and proclaiming his own great acts of courage. He himself writes letters to frighten Hezekiah and his people to surrender the city.

His tactics were of mean nature in order to terrify the common people and persuade them to desert Hezekiah.

Sennacherib, the blasphemer and a proud king compared our living God, the Maker of heaven and earth, with the idol-gods of the nations. He treated the work of men's hands more than the works of living God. He had a great contempt for our God. Addressing Hezekiah's people he says:

Now therefore let not Hezekiah deceive you, nor persuade you in this way, neither yet believe him: for no god of any nation or kingdom was able to deliver his people out of my hand, and out of the hand of my fathers: how much less shall your God deliver you out of my hand? (2 Chronicles 32:15)

Sennacherib had blasphemed the living God and fancifully ridiculed the living God as the God of Israel only. His rude and impertinent and intemperate behavior filled with profane attitude was the reason for his downfall and punishment.

Yes! Here comes the downfall of Sennacherib, the proud king. The Lord sent an angel who destroyed everyone in the Sennacherib's camp and saved Hezekiah and the inhabitants of Jerusalem from his hand.

Thereafter many brought gifts unto the Lord to Jerusalem and gifts to Hezekiah, who was magnified in the sight of all the nations from then on.

And for this cause Hezekiah the king, and the prophet Isaiah the son of Amoz, prayed and cried to heaven. And the LORD sent an angel, who cut off all the mighty men of valor, and the leaders and captains in the camp of the king of Assyria. So he returned with shame of face to his own land.

And when he had come into the house of his god, sons that came forth of his own body struck him down there with the sword (cf. 2 Chronicles 32:20-21)

The proud king of Assyria was defeated by the Lord and humble king Hezekiah was exalted. Those who take refuge in the Lord will find victory in him and respect in the sight of men.

Thus the LORD saved Hezekiah and the inhabitants of Jerusalem from the hand of Sennacherib the king of Assyria, and from the hand of all others, and guided them on every side. And many brought gifts unto the LORD to Jerusalem, and precious gifts to Hezekiah king of Judah: so that he was magnified in the sight of all nations from that time on. (2 Chronicles 32:22-23)

DAY 16 EVERYTHING IS DUNG

Everything in this world is 'dung'

In the Old Testament the instructions given by God to Abraham to circumcise every male child on the eighth day was a covenant between God and Abraham. (A covenant is a mutual agreement).

God said every male child among the seed of Abraham after him, whether he is born in the house, or bought with money of any stranger, one that is not of Abraham's seed shall be circumcised and if anyone was not circumcised that soul shall be cut off from his people. It was equivalent to breaking the covenant.

This covenant was established by God between Him and Abraham that He will be God of Abraham and his posterity through Isaac. God promised Abraham that He will give him the land of Canaan as an everlasting possession. (Genesis 17:7-9)

For a New Testament believer circumcision profits nothing. Apostle Paul emphasized this fact in Romans 2:25 "For circumcision verily profiteth, if thou keep the law: but if thou be a breaker of the law, thy circumcision is made uncircumcision".

Referring to this circumcision, Apostle Paul writes in Philippians 3:4-8 that he was from the stock of Israel, of the tribe of Benjamin, a Pharisee, circumcised on the eighth day. He says that if anyone has more trust in circumcision he would consider himself a better man than any other for having kept the law. He writes that, before he accepted Jesus as his Lord, he had great zeal to persecute the Church.

Paul's name was Saul before his conversion to follow Jesus. Perhaps, Paul would have gained wealth, name and fame if only he continued that which he was doing and in his status as a Pharisee, of the tribe of Benjamin, and with the pride of having been circumcised.

However, God's plan was not to let Paul into the world to earn some temporal benefits in this world, but His plan was to use Paul for His glory.

Paul says that he counted all the gain that he had in this world, or that which he would have had in this world by not accepting Jesus as his Savior was of no gain. He says it was all waste and loss.

The only thing that counted for him as gain was the excellence of the knowledge of Lord Jesus Christ, whom he called, as 'my Lord'. Paul calls everything of this world is just 'dung', a refuse.

"Yea doubtless, and I count all things but loss for the excellency of the knowledge of Christ Jesus my Lord: for whom I have suffered the loss of all things, and do count them but dung, that I may win Christ" (Philippians 3:8)

DAY 17 GOD LOVES HIS PEOPLE

"And I saw thrones, and they sat upon them, and judgment was given unto them: and I saw the souls of them that were beheaded for the witness of Jesus, and for the word of God, and which had not worshipped the beast, neither his image, neither had received his mark upon their foreheads, or in their hands; and they lived and reigned with Christ a thousand years" (Revelation 20:4)

God promised Abraham that in Isaac will be the blessed people who will be His people and He will be their God. Jesus came to save the children of Israel, yet they rejected him. This paved the way for Gentiles to come to him for salvation and secure God's mercy.

All those who had believed Jesus as their savior and laid faith in him were saved and likewise all those who believe in him shall be saved. Two thieves were crucified one on either side of Lord Jesus.

One of them mocked Jesus while the other sought mercy from Jesus. He prayed that Jesus may remember him when He comes in his Kingdom. Jesus said to the thief who prayed for mercy that he would be in Paradise the very same day when Jesus died on the cross. Jesus was buried and he rose from the dead on the third day and later ascended into heaven. He is seated on the right hand of the Father in heaven. He will come soon. Salvation is available to anyone who calls upon Jesus for mercy.

Isaiah 40:11 "He shall feed his flock like a shepherd: he shall gather the lambs with his arm, and carry [them] in his bosom, [and] shall gently lead those that are with young".

Israel has become one nation in 1948 but they do not have the shepherd yet. They rejected Jesus as their Messiah and called for his blood to be upon them.

Has God forgotten Israel because they rejected him as their Messiah? No. God said "Can a woman forget her sucking child, that she should not have compassion on the son of her womb? yea, they may forget, yet will I not forget thee". Isaiah 49:15.

The things are going to be worse for them that they will call for help from Jesus. He would not come until they realize that they have rejected him and they need him. They will face terrible persecution under Antichrist in the last days. They would cry that the mountains may fall on them and kill them (Rev.6:16). Israel will call upon God during the Great Tribulation period. God is not going to leave them but he will bring them on their knees to call upon his help. Then shall the Lord come to them and be their King of kings and Lord of lords. Jesus will reign for thousand years from the throne of David.

And I will give them an heart to know me, that I am the LORD: and they shall be my people, and I will be their God: for they shall return unto me with their whole heart. (Jeremiah 24:7)

God loved His people but they kept on rejecting him. The consequences, as Paul says, would be:

Tribulation and anguish, upon every soul of man that doeth evil, of the Jew first, and also of the Gentile; (Romans 2:9)

But, all those whose sins are washed in the blood of Jesus, irrespective of Jews or Gentiles will be caught up together to meet the Lord in the air even before the Great Tribulation starts.

"The dead shall rise first and we who are alive and remain shall be caught up together with them in the clouds to meet the Lord in the air: and so shall be ever be with the Lord" (1 Thessalonians 4:16-17)

Apostle Paul writes "For there is no difference between the Jew and the Greek: for the same Lord over all is rich unto all that call upon him". (Romans 10:12)

It is the Church that stands above Jew or Gentile finally and his saints as the bride of Jesus and as the Church that is going to be precious possession of Lord Jesus Christ.

DAY 18 HE IS RISEN

"And when the sabbath was past, Mary Magdalene, and Mary the mother of James, and Salome, had bought sweet spices, that they might come and anoint him. And very early in the morning the first day of the week, they came unto the sepulcher at the rising of the sun. And they said among themselves, Who shall roll us away the stone from the door of the sepulcher? And when they looked, they saw that the stone was rolled away: for it was very great". (Mark 16:1-4)

On the day when Jesus was tried before Pontius Pilate the governor, there was option for people to have either Jesus released or Barabbas released. It was feast day and according to their custom a prisoner of their choice could be released.

Pilate asked the people as to whom they prefer to be released; whether it was Barabbas or Jesus. The people cried that Barabbas, a notable criminal be released in preference to that of innocent Jesus. (Matthew 27:15-18)

Pilate knew that Jesus was innocent and that is why he asked the people as to what evil Jesus had committed. A great politician as he was, Pontius Pilate did not want to offend Herod on one side and the people on the other. But the people cried more that Jesus should be crucified. "And the governor said, why, what evil has he done? But they cried out the more, saying, Let him be crucified". (Matthew 27:23)

Then Pilate washed his hands and justified himself saying: "I am innocent of the blood of this just person: see you to it". (Matthew 27:24) Pilate acknowledged that Jesus was just person, yet he has handed over Jesus to the choice of people. Thus Pilate is guilty of not showing the justice.

A rich man of Arimathaea, named Joseph, who also himself was Jesus' disciple begged for the body of Jesus and he laid it in his own new tomb.

And laid it in his own new tomb, which he had hewn out in the rock: and he rolled a great stone to the door of the sepulchre, and departed. (Matthew 27:60)

On the tomb, where the dead body of Jesus was laid, a great stone was rolled over it. The tomb was closed with that great stone and it was sealed so that no one could remove the body of Jesus or steal the body of Jesus.

All the accusers took care that the dead body of Jesus was not removed from the tomb. The tomb was guarded so that no one could remove or steal the body of Jesus.

"Pilate said unto them, You have guards: go your way, make it as sure as you can. So they went, and made the sepulcher sure, sealing the stone, and setting a guard". (Matthew 27:65-66)

But then, as per the prophecy and as Jesus told beforehand, he rose from the dead and went to Galilee before Mary Magdalene and Mary the mother of James reached the tomb.

After the Sabbath was past early in the morning Mary Magdalene, and Mary the mother of James went to the tomb where Jesus was laid. Jesus had told that he will rise on the third day, and yet these two missed the timing very badly. Not only this, but before they reached the tomb, they had a big question in their minds as to who will role away the stone?

However they found answer to their question when the Angel of the Lord announced that he was risen from the dead.

And, behold, there was a great earthquake: for the angel of the Lord descended from heaven, and came and rolled back the stone from the door, and sat upon it. (Matthew 28:2)

"And the angel answered and said unto the women, Fear not: for I know that you seek Jesus, who was crucified. He is not here: for he is risen, as he said. Come, see the place where the Lord lay" (Matthew 28:5-6)

DAY 19 HEAVEN REJOICES

"I say unto you, that likewise joy shall be in heaven over one sinner that repenteth, more than over ninety and nine just persons, which need no repentance". (Luke 15:7)

There are three things seen in the parable of the lost sheep described in Luke 15:1-7. Firstly, Jesus is seen to be receiving publicans and sinners. Secondly, Jesus is seen questioning as to what man is he who does not leave ninety nine of his sheep to go in search of one lost sheep. Thirdly, when the man finds the lost sheep he is seen rejoicing over the one lost and found sheep.

At the outset it is seen that publicans and sinners drew near unto him. There could be at least three reasons why publicans and sinners drew near unto him. One could be that Jesus was doing miracles, healing the sick; the second could be that his message was powerful and many were being either saved or impressed and the third could be to trap him in one question or the other.

The publicans are tax collectors, who were a hated lot among the Jews of the day. They were in close association with noted sinners, perhaps, harlots, of the day. These two went near unto Jesus to hear as to what Jesus had to say. The Pharisees and the Scribes, highly educated lot of those days, accused Jesus of having concern for the publicans and sinners.

Jesus answers them in parable and questions them as to who would not leave ninety nine of his sheep that are secure in order to search for one lost sheep of his own. Jesus says that after the man finds the lost sheep he rejoices over it, rather than saying any complaints about it going astray.

Here is seen the love of God, who sent his one and only Son, Jesus Christ in search of the lost sinners. When the lost sinner is found he rejoices over him/her; rather than recording any complaint against him.

When the Father sees one, who has repented of his sin, he sees only the blood of His Son that cleansed the sin and the crystal clear image of the repented sinner. He does not see or remember sins of any one, who confesses them to God in Jesus name.

"Come now, and let us reason together, saith the LORD: though your sins be as scarlet, they shall be as white as snow; though they be red like crimson, they shall be as wool" (Isaiah 1:18)

DAY 20 GOD CARES

The children of Israel had sweet water at Marah and good rest at Elim. After that they resumed they journey and reached the wilderness of Sin. There, they murmured against God for food. They had earlier murmured for water and rest and God provided sweet water and good rest, yet they now complain for food. They had lost their confidence that God would provide their needs.

Not only have they complained that they did not have food, but they remembered the food that they had in Egypt when they were slaves. They spoke as if they were happy under Pharaoh and the food that Pharaoh gave to them was good enough.

They soon forgot their liberation from slavery and they soon forgot that they were heading to a promised land, which according to God, was a land of milk and honey.

 The LORD then said to Moses that he will rain heavenly bread for them and people should go out and gather the food only to the extent that was needed for them for the day. The LORD also told them that on the sixth day they should collect heavenly bread for the seventh day also, so that they may take rest on the seventh day.

Moses and Aaron said to the children of Israel that they will know who the LORD that brought them out of Egypt was.

Aaron spoke to the children of Israel as instructed by Moses and as he was yet speaking the glory of the LORD appeared in the cloud and spoke to Moses saying, "I have heard the murmurings of the children of Israel: speak unto them, saying,

At even ye shall eat flesh, and in the morning ye shall be filled with bread; and ye shall know that I am the LORD your God" (Exodus 16:12)

"And it came to pass, that at even the quails came up, and covered the camp: and in the morning the dew lay round about the host". (Exodus 16:13)

When the dew disappeared there appeared on the "face of the wilderness a small round thing as the hoar frost on the ground". The children of Israel saw the wonderful food and did not know what it was; and they called it as, "Manna".

Moses said to them that it was the heavenly bread that the LORD gave them to eat. There was a measure, "Omer" given to them and they were not allowed to gather more than that a day. He, who gathered much more than 'Omer' had nothing more and he, who had gathered less had no lack of it, because everyone gathered according to one's need for the day.

Here man's true nature is revealed to do that which he was not supposed to do. Some in the camp did not obey what Moses said to them, and gathered more food for the day than what was required; but surprisingly the excess food perished.

The food that they gathered on the sixth day for the seventh day did not perish, but lasted as fresh as it was gathered on the same day.

The "Manna" was like coriander seed, white and tasty like wafers made with honey. God takes care of His children. God chastised the children of Israel for murmuring against him yet he took care of them.

Psalmist said:

"I have been young, and now am old; yet have I not seen the righteous forsaken, nor his seed begging bread". (Psalms 37:25)

DAY 21 JACOB'S TROUBLE

Alas! for that day is great, so that none is like it: it is even the time of Jacob's trouble; but he shall be saved out of it. (Jeremiah 30:7)

What do the Scriptures say about Jacob's trouble?

The time of Jacob's trouble, is the time of 'great tribulation' when Israel will mourn for the Lord, whom they crucified and this will make a way for the national repentance. God will have mercy on Israel and will restore to them their lost kingdom.

The second coming of Jesus as seen by the left- behind Jews and unbelievers is the second appearance of Lord Jesus Christ on this earth. Then the feet of Lord Jesus stand upon the Mount Olives and thereafter He will rule for one thousand years literally from the throne of David.

The Lord is jealous God, and He shall not tolerate any one, who worships the idols, much less he tolerated the children of Israel. The troubles and curses they heaped upon themselves by worshipping idols, and making graven images and by doing evil things in the sight of the Lord God, provoked him to anger.

God swore saying, "...I call heaven and earth to witness against you this day that ye shall soon utterly perish from off the land whereunto ye go over Jordan to possess it; ye shall not prolong your days upon it, but shall utterly be destroyed. And the LORD shall scatter you among the nations, and ye shall be left few in

number among the heathen, whither the LORD shall lead you."
(Deuteronomy 4:24-27)

Even though they are scattered yet if they repent of their sins
and call upon God as their Savior, He said He will deliver from
the tribulation and gather them as one nation.

The great tribulation will be such as was never before in the
whole history of mankind upon this earth, and this is the time
when the children of Israel will surely confess that the Lord
Jesus is their Messiah, and God will not go back on His words of
restoring them their land, and every one's name will be found in
the 'book'. (Dan.12:1)

Even though many Israelites have returned to their land, and
also the nation of Israel was declared independent on May 15th,
1948, yet the complete gathering of the tribes from northern
kingdom that were scattered after the Assyrians had taken
them captive and the tribes from southern kingdom, who were
taken captive by Babylonians, and thereafter by Persians is not
complete.

Also, the children of Israel living in Israel are not all saved. God
will use 'great tribulation', which comes under 'the time of
Jacob's trouble', for calling upon their Savior, Lord Jesus as their
Messiah.

God warned beforehand that when they are in tribulation, and
when all those troubles come upon them in the latter days, and
if they turn to the Lord God, and be obedient to Him, He will not

forget the covenant that He made with Abraham, Isaac, and Jacob and swore to them. (Ref. Deut. 4:30, 31).

In Deut. 30:1-3 God said, that when Israel realizes that He had driven them out of their country for the sins they committed, and call upon Him for mercy, obey His voice according to all that He had commanded, He will have compassion on them and gather them from all the nations, where He had scattered them.

DAY 22 NEW NAME FOR JERUSALEM

The Holy city Jerusalem, the city of our Lord, is now desolate and not in good shape. The city is forsaken and destroyed. But, the day will come when the city will be called "Hephzibah", and its land "Beulah".

The Lord delights in making the city delightful for everyone and the land like married woman. (Isaiah Ch. 62:4). This is a prophecy about the status of Jerusalem in the millennial kingdom of Jesus.

Lord Jesus Christ is the Messiah. The Jews rejected him and called upon themselves the blood of Jesus in order that he may be crucified (Matthew 27:24-25). Peter's speech testifies about those who crucified Jesus.

"Ye men of Israel, hear these words; Jesus of Nazareth, a man approved of God among you by miracles and wonders and signs, which God did by him in the midst of you, as ye yourselves also know: Him, being delivered by the determinate counsel and foreknowledge of God, ye have taken, and by wicked hands have crucified and slain" (Acts 2:22-23)

Indeed, they paid the price in AD 70 according to historians. Earlier, they worshipped idols many-a-time and were chastised by God. They rebelled against God and paid the price for their actions. Yet, they are his people; the city of David is his city.

Like Boaz, who was kinsman redeemer of Ruth, Jesus is our redeemer. He came into this world, died for our sins, was buried, rose from the dead on the third day and later ascended into heaven. He is seated on the right hand of the Majesty and interceding for us.

We, who are redeemed by the blood of Christ, are greater than the unrepentant Jews. But for those, who have accepted Jesus as their personal savior, there is no condemnation irrespective of their race, ethnicity, color, or creed.

Lord Jesus, who is the messiah, speaks and says that he will not sit quite, nor will he rest until he redeems city of Jerusalem again. He defeats the kings loyal to Antichrist at "Armageddon", and sits on the throne of David and literally rules.

In the thousand years of his rule there shall be perfect peace. Satan will be bound with chains and thrown into abyss by an angel who comes from heaven. Later Satan will be released for a short time when he goes Gog and Maggot to deceive the nations but fire from God comes down from heaven and devours Satan. (Revelation Ch. 20:8) The dead who did not accept Jesus Christ as their personal savior will resurrect at that time.

The Lord shall judge them at the 'Great white throne' and cast them along with death, hell, and the devil and his angels into the 'lake of fire' to be tormented for ever and ever. This is the second death.

For those who are saved, there is no second death but they will have everlasting life to be with the Lord for ever and ever. Note here when Antichrist and false prophet are thrown into the lake of fire! It is before the devil that deceived!!! Revelation 20:10 confirms it.

When the devil was cast into the lake of fire, the Antichrist and the false prophet were already there in the lake of fire.

These are only the ones who will be in the lake of fire before the 'Great White Throne Judgment' (Revelation 16:16 and Revelation 20:8-10). Does the Scripture say anybody is thrown into the lake of fire before Antichrist and false prophet. No, not at all!

 There shall come out of heaven a New Jerusalem and we, who are saved, shall be in that Holy City. The Church is the bride of our Lord Jesus Christ. Lord Jesus says that he has set watchmen upon the walls of Jerusalem and they will not keep quite nor will sleep but keep a watch over the city and will make the city a praise of the earth.

This is a promise of Messiah and he has sworn by his right hand and by the arm of his strength. Messiah promised that no more the enemies of Jerusalem will eat its corn as their food no stranger will ever drink its wine. Gentiles will see its righteousness and kings will glory.

 "And the Gentiles shall see thy righteousness, and all kings thy glory: and thou shalt be called by a new name, which the mouth of the LORD shall name." (Isaiah 62:2)

DEVOTIONALS FOR TWO MONTHS

DAY 23 JESUS AND HIS EARTHLY RELATIVES

What was the importance that the relatives of Jesus had on this earth?

On seeing the miracles that Jesus did and the words of wisdom that he spoke to the people, a woman said that the mother who bore Jesus as her son was blessed. The woman adored Mary, the blessed woman, who was the earthly mother of Jesus.

In her own thoughts the woman, who bore Jesus as her son was blessed. Her focus was mainly on the mother, who bore Jesus as her son. In the same chapter (Luke 11), where this woman is shown as having said that the woman who bore Jesus was blessed, indeed there were some important points to take note of.

Firstly, it was about the prayer that Jesus taught his disciples.

Secondly, it was an insistent entreaty of a friend in need seeking help from his friend, and how impossible it is that the heavenly Father would give a serpent to the one, who asks him bread.

Thirdly, it was about casting of a devil that showed that Jesus was divine. The woman then said as it is written in Luke 1:27 "And it came to pass, as he space these things, a certain woman of the company lifted up her voice, and said unto him, Blessed is the womb that bare thee, and the paps which thou hast sucked." Jesus responded "But he said, Yea rather, blessed are they that hear the word of God, and keep it". (Luke 11:28)

Mary the earthly mother of Jesus was indeed a blessed woman. The angel of the Lord said that Mary found favor with God, and that she shall bring forth a son, and that she shall call his name JESUS, because he shall save his people from their sins. (Matthew 1:21, Luke 1:30) But that which was conceived in her was of the Holy Ghost. (Matthew 1:20)

When Mary the mother of Jesus and his half-brothers had concern for him "...he looked round about on them which sat about him, and said, Behold my mother and my brethren! For whosoever shall do the will of God, the same is my brother, and my sister, and mother. (Mark 3:34-35) His half-brothers did not believe that Jesus was the Son of God, until after his resurrection. (John 7:5).

The people around him wondered if he was not the carpenter's son, and if his mother was not Mary, or his brothers James, Joses, Simon, and Judas (Jude) (Matthew 13:55)

But, after the crucifixion and resurrection of Lord Jesus Christ, the earthly mother of Jesus and his half-brothers realized that Jesus was not a mere man, but He was their Savior, just as he was of many. Therefore, Mary the mother of Jesus joined his half-brothers, and others including the women, who are saved and continued with one accord in prayer and supplication. (Acts 1:14)

Mary the earthly mother was a blessed woman, who found favor in the sight of God, but she was not the one who deserved our worship. She needed a Savior, and the Savior was Jesus. She prayed to God, and Lord Jesus was her God.

DAY 24 MANSIONS FOR US

"In my Father's house are many mansions: if it were not so, I would have told you. I go to prepare a place for you" John 14:2

Lord Jesus Christ's purpose of coming again to this earth is two-fold; firstly the second coming is for receiving His own to Himself, and secondly to fulfill the promises made to Israel. Church consisting of saved ones constitutes His bride.

The marriage of the bride takes place according to Scriptures after the Church is caught up in the clouds to meet the Lord in the air. To this marriage between the Lord and His bride are not invited the unsaved ones. Lord Jesus Christ promised mansions for His Children, who believe in Him.

Jesus promised that He was going to heaven to prepare mansions for believers in Him. This promise is given in John 14:2 and 3 and this purpose, which was a mystery in the Old Testament, is revealed in the New Testament.

The earthly blessings promised to the children of Israel will be restored unto them when Lord Jesus Christ appears on this earth, while the heavenly blessings promised to His bride are given after the Church is caught up in the clouds to meet the Lord in the air.

After seven years period, when Antichrist rules the earth, and the unbelievers, and Jews, who persecuted Him, undergo God's wrath, Jesus stands on the Mount olives, and later He rules literally for one thousand years sitting on the throne of David fulfilling the prophesies. The believers constituting His Bride will be always with the Lord.

The Church consisting of heavenly ones, saved in the precious blood of Lord Jesus Christ is His precious bride. His bride consisting of blessed ones should not be confused with the Israel.

The covenants made to the children of Israel will be fulfilled on this earth. (Ref: Acts 1:6, Hebrews 9:28 and Romans 11:28, etc.). Israel and the Church are separate and this fact is to be understood clearly.

And he said unto them, It is not for you to know the times or the seasons, which the Father hath put in his own power. (Acts 1:7)

DAY 25 WE ARE SAFE

JESUS SAVES YOU

Then touched he their eyes, saying, According to your faith be it unto you. (Matthew 9:29)

The blind receive their sight, and the lame walk, the lepers are cleansed, and the deaf hear, the dead are raised up, and the poor have the gospel preached to them. (Matthew 11:5)

Even though Jesus did miracles, yet Jews, who usually took delight in miracles, did not believe on Him as their Messiah, because they thought their Messiah would come like a king in a royal family. Contrary to their expectations Jesus was born as a poor man in the womb of Virgin Mary conceived of the Holy Ghost.

After Jesus grew up and started his ministry at the age of about thirty he chose few and called them to be his disciples. One such disciple was Matthew, who was a Publican; he collected customs and tax.

Jews hated tax collectors because they were, in collaboration with authorities, harassing them. But then, this tax collector, Matthew, found grace in the sight of the Lord, and he was called to be one of his disciples. Matthew willingly accepted the calling from Jesus and instantly responded by following him.

At one point of time, when Jesus was sitting with tax collectors and sinners, Pharisees, a learned sect of Jews, questioned him as to why he was sitting with them to eat. When Jesus heard that question, he answered and said that those who are healthy do not need a physician, but they that are sick need physician. That was to tell them that the righteous do not need Savior, but sinners do need Savior.

Basically, Jesus came for his own people, that is, the Jews; but then the salvation is extended to Gentiles also because Jews rejected Jesus as their "Messiah".

The miracles that Jesus would do were prophesied in Isaiah 35:5-6 "Then the eyes of the blind shall be opened, and the ears of the deaf shall be unstopped. Then shall the lame man leap as an hart, and the tongue of the dumb sing: for in the wilderness shall waters break out, and streams in the desert".

The prophecy was fulfilled when Jesus healed the sick. God said to the children of Israel through Moses that if they "hearkened diligently to the LORD", the Lord would not bring upon them any of the diseases that He brought upon Egyptians (Exodus 15:26). But they disobeyed God several times and their disobedience needed reconciliation.

Adam rebelled against God by transgressing the commandment of God. Bible records that we are all sinners by birth and there is no one righteous.

According to 1 John 1:8 "If we say that we have no sin, we deceive ourselves, and the truth is not in us". The Children of Israel transgressed the commandments of God several times.

In order to reconcile man with God, the Son of God, Jesus came into this world in the form of man to take upon our sins on him and die in our place that whosoever believes on him shall receive salvation and be saved from eternal damnation.

God loved man so much that He gave his one and only Son, Jesus Christ that whoever believes in him shall be saved.

Friend, are you burdened with the thought that your sin is too great that it cannot be forgiven? Please be sure that every sin, except blasphemy of the Holy Spirit, is pardonable by God.

"Come unto me, all ye that labour and are heavy laden, and I will give you rest" (Matthew 11:28)

DAY 26 JOSPEH FORGIVES

"And his brothers also went and fell down before his face; and they said, Behold, we are your servants. And Joseph said unto them, Fear not: for am I in the place of God? But as for you, you thought evil against me; but God meant it unto good, to bring to pass, as it is this day, to save many people alive". (Genesis 50:18-20)

Joseph's brothers did not like the interpretations Joseph gave of the dreams he dreamt.

Joseph's father rebuked him when he interpreted his second dream.

Joseph's brothers felt jealous of Joseph and conspired to do harm to Joseph.

"And they said one to another, Behold, this dreamer comes. Come now therefore, and let us slay him, and cast him into some pit, and we will say, Some evil beast has devoured him: and we shall see what will become of his dreams". (Genesis 37:19-20)

Joseph's brothers cast Joseph in a waterless pit. Later he was pulled out by Midianites who sold him to Ishmaelites, who in turn, sold him to the Egyptians. Joseph proved himself worthy of his calling by escaping from the seduction of Potiphar's wife. Joseph remained true and honest to his master, Potiphar. Things did not seem to be going in favor of Joseph, when he was trying to escape from the trouble. He actually got in to the trouble when Potiphar's wife accused him of molesting her. His master gave credence to his wife and sent Joseph in to prison.

Later, when Joseph interpreted Pharaoh's dreams he was released from the prison and Pharaoh made him governor in the land of Egypt. He had great authority in Egypt.

"And Pharaoh said unto Joseph, Since God has showed you all this, there is none so discreet and wise as you are: You shall be over my house, and according unto your word shall all my people be ruled: only in the throne will I be greater than you". (Genesis 41:39-40)

"And Pharaoh said unto Joseph, I am Pharaoh, and without you shall no man lift up his hand or foot in all the land of Egypt". (Genesis 41:44)

In spite of having all the authority on his side, Joseph acknowledged in Chapter 45:8 "So then, it was not you who sent me here, but god. He made me father to Pharaoh, lord of his entire household and ruler of all Egypt."

Let us turn to Luke Chapter 23 verse 34 Jesus said, "Father forgive them, for they do not know what they are doing…"

How great is the love of Jesus Christ, the Savior of this world. While chief priests and the teachers of the law, who were standing near the cross of Calvary, accusing the Son of God, Jesus Christ, While Herod and his soldiers were ridiculing him and mocked him, Oh! Then, Jesus said," Father forgive them, for they do not know what they are doing…"

The people there were representatives of all of us. We were all crucifying Jesus on the cross of Calvary. We all nailed his palms to the hard cross, and crowned him with crown of thorns

Should we not receive him as our savior and acknowledge him as our Lord? Yes, Jesus is the Lord. He is the savior. Let us worship him in spirit and truth.

DAY 27 THE JUDGMENT OF NATIONS

The Sheep and Goat Judgment

After Antichrist's seven-year period is over Lord Jesus Christ descends and steps on the Mount of Olives. "And his feet shall stand in that day upon the mount of Olives, which is before Jerusalem on the east, and the mount of Olives shall cleave in the midst thereof toward the east and toward the west, and there shall be a very great valley; and half of the mountain shall remove toward the north, and half of it toward the south". (Zechariah 14:4)

All nations (gentiles) will be gathered unto Lord Jesus and He sits on the throne of glory. He will separate saved from the unsaved ones just as shepherd divides his sheep from the goats. (Ref. Matthew 25:32). These are not the ones who were already 'caught up' to be with the Lord for ever and ever at 'rapture'.

The word 'sheep' refers to the saved ones, who had their salvation during the period, when the Lord with His chaste bride is in the mid-air, and likewise the word 'goats' refers to the unsaved ones.

The King, who is our Lord and Savior Jesus Christ, will say unto those, who are on His right hand side, 'Come, ye blessed of my Father' and then, the King will say unto those, who are on his left hand side, 'Depart from me, ye cursed, into everlasting fire, prepared for devil and his angels'.

The words of the King at this judgment are very sharp and shrewd. To those, who are on His right hand side, the King will say that when He was hungry they gave Him meat, and when He was thirsty they gave Him drink, and when he was a stranger they took care of Him; Naked, and they clothed Him, and when He was sick they visited Him, when He was in prison, they went to see Him.

The righteous on the right side of the King will be filled with the surprise and ask the King, when was He hungry, thirsty, naked, sick and in prison. "And the King shall answer and say unto them, Verily I say unto you, Inasmuch as ye have done it unto one of the least of these my brethren, ye have done it unto me". (Matthew 25:40)

Similarly, the King will say very sharp and shrewd words to those, who are on His left side, that they did not give Him food when He was hungry, that they did not give him water when He was thirsty, that they did not receive Him in when He was stranger, that they did not clothe him when He was naked, that they did not visit Him when He was sick, and that they did not minister unto Him when He was in prison.

Those, whom the Word of God, calls as 'goats', (unsaved) ones, ask Him surprisingly, when they did not gave Him drink, food, and when was He naked that they did not clothe Him, and when was He stranger that they did not take Him in, and when He was sick that they did not minister unto Him, and when was in prison that they did not minister unto Him.

"Then shall he answer them, saying, Verily I say unto you, Inasmuch as ye did it not to one of the least of these, ye did it not to me" (Matthew 25:45)

The blessings that the King shall give unto the righteous are that they will 'inherit the kingdom prepared for you from the foundation of the world' and the punishment the King renders unto those, who are not saved will be 'Depart from me, ye cursed, into everlasting fire, prepared for the devil and his angels'.

DAY 28 THE JUDGMENT SEAT OF CHRIST

"For we must all appear before the judgment seat of Christ; that every one may receive the things done in his body, according to that he hath done, whether it be good or bad". (2 Corinthians 5:10)

Every believer has to account for the deeds he has done on this earth in order to receive the rewards at the Judgment seat of Christ. The judgment seat of Christ is also known as 'Bema seat of Christ'.

Although the phrase 'Bema seat of Christ' is not in the Bible, this word is commonly used in Christian parlance just as the word "Trinity" is used for Triune God – The Father, The Son and The Holy Spirit. The believer in Christ shall stand at the judgment seat of Christ not as the one to receive judgment for punishment, but for receiving the rewards he is entitled for working for the Lord.

"For the Lord himself shall descend from heaven with a shout, with the voice of the archangel, and with the trump of God: and the dead in Christ shall rise first: Then we which are alive and remain shall be caught up together with them in the clouds, to meet the Lord in the air: and so shall we ever be with the Lord". (1 Thessalonians 4:16-17)

During the period of time when the believer is with the Lord and after being 'caught up' which is usually called as the "rapture", the Lord will honor his servant for the service he rendered unto Him when he was on this earth.

We are not to judge our brothers because we shall all stand before the judgment seat of Christ (Rom.14:10). The time will come when the Lord comes and He brings to the light every hidden things of darkness, and will show the counsels that have taken place in the hearts. While God does this in the presence of every believer at the judgment seat of Christ every man will praise God (1 Cor.4:5).

Lord Jesus Christ is our life and He will appear in the clouds in glory to receive His own unto Himself and honor them with rewards.

This judgment seat of Christ is not the Great white Throne judgment about which there is reference in Revelation Chapter 20:14 when those, who have not believed in Him, will be judged.

These unbelievers will have their everlasting destiny in the lake of fire to be tormented day in and day out for ever and ever along with the Satan and his angels. The judgment seat of Christ is the raised seat where Lord Jesus sits as the King of kings to administer justice.

There shall be no condemnation for the believers, who are in Christ, and who have not walked after the flesh, but sought to walk after the Spirit. (Rom 8:1). The believers will not face judgment at 'Great white throne' mentioned in Revelation Chapter 20:11

God was in Christ and reconciled us unto Himself, and made us, who have trusted in Him, and confessed our sins to Him, as his heirs and did not impute our trespasses unto us, but washed our sins in the precious blood of Jesus.

We are His workmanship, created in Christ unto good works and we stand worthy of our calling and deserve our rewards at the 'Bema Seat of Christ'. It is a blessed hope for believer that he will be honored for putting on Christ and for living holy life.

It is at this time, when we, the believers are with the Lord, that we will be rewarded before He reveals Himself on this earth again.

DAY 29 LAW AND GRACE

"My little children, of whom I travail in birth again until Christ be formed in you" (Galatians 4:19)

Paul's feels as if he was under the travail of child birth to explain to Galatians the difference between law and grace, and how hard it is to be under law rather than accept 'grace' alone as the way for salvation. He calls them, now, 'my little children', and tries to explain to them about the implications in believing that law and works only would save them.

Galatians were under the erroneous belief that law and works only can save them. They desired to take pride in a list of rules they prescribed for them and thought if they keep the law and rules then they would consider them as perfect.

That, in other words, renders a notion that man can earn his own salvation by keeping a set of rules, like being good and doing good etc. These things help men to be good men but would not secure salvation that is available free of cost as a result of belief in the works of Jesus, the Son of God, did for men.

Jesus came down into this world to redeem us from the bondage of sin, and, therefore, took upon himself, our transgressions and died for our sake. The fruits of the Holy Spirit are love, joy, peace, longsuffering, gentleness, goodness, faith, Meekness, temperance. A saved man will have in him the Spirit of God and will have the fruits of the Holy Spirit.

However, possession of these good qualities without accepting Jesus as 'Lord' will not make us a man eligible to have eternal life. The only way to have eternal life is to believe in the efficacy of the blood of Jesus Christ and accept the fact that he died in our stead on the cross.

Paul explains to Galatians, just as a matured man explaining to children that all those who believe that law can save them are like those, who are of 'bondwoman' and all those who believe in the 'grace' of Jesus are like those, who are of free woman. He quotes from Old Testament the things that have happened in Abram's life as described in Genesis 16th Chapter.

Sarai sent her handmaid, Hagar to sleep with Abram, and a son was born. It was legalism on the part of Sarai and Abram a method that finds a way out for them. Later a son was born to Abraham and his wife Sarah as a consequence of the promise of God to them.

This son of the promise of God was of faith in God and His grace. The son, who was born to Hagar, was of the flesh, and the son born of promise to Sarai, was blessed.

The posterity of bondwoman is still under bondage of Mosaic Law and the posterity of the free woman, who is supposed to be free from the bondage of Mosaic Law, have unfortunately, embraced the law and works as their way for salvation, rejected Messiah as their Savior, and is still under the bondage of law.

The legalists still insist that it is right to be under the law and keep the law to be saved. Such legalism will lead to the belief that there is no justification by the grace of God, but their own works will lead them to have eternal life.

"So then, brethren, we are not children of the bondwoman, but of the free". (Galatians 4:31)

"Christ is become of no effect unto you, whosoever of you are justified by the law; ye are fallen from grace". (Galatians 5:4)

DAY 30 LET US BE BLESSED

"Blessed is the man that walketh not in the counsel of the ungodly, nor standeth in the way of sinners, nor sitteth in the seat of the scornful". (Psalms 1:1)

In Psalm Chapter 1the Psalmist mentions about three categories of people. He mentions firstly about the ungodly, secondly about sinners, and thirdly about scorners and he says that those who do not walk in the counsel of the ungodly and those who do not stand in the way of sinners, or sit in the seat of the scornful are blessed.

The godly ways are honoring God and walking in his ways. In Joshua Chapter 1 verse 8 The Lord said to Joshua that the word of God should not depart out of his mouth, but he should meditate therein day in and day out and do according to what is written therein. The way to be prosperous and be blessed is that way as shown by the Lord.

"This book of the law shall not depart out of thy mouth; but thou shalt meditate therein day and night, that thou mayest observe to do according to all that is written therein: for then thou shalt make thy way prosperous, and then thou shalt have good success" (Joshua 1:8)

The man who stands in the way of the sinners has inclination always to commit sin. The temptations are numerous and Satan does not lack the ingenuity needed to attack a person who stands in the way of sinners. To be among sinners is like being constantly in contact with infected persons. If sufficient precautions are not taken the entire time the infection spreads to healthy person. The person sitting in the scornful has always the possibilities of making scorn of salvation, God, and truth. There are those who say there is no God. There are those who say they do everything by their own intelligence.

"Be not deceived; God is not mocked: for whatsoever a man soweth, that shall he also reap" (Galatians 6:7)

Apostle Paul writes about the ungodly who lived during Noah's period. The ungodly increased in number in the days of Noah wherefore God punished the whole world with huge deluge but saved Noah, who was a preacher of righteousness, and saved his family.

"And spared not the old world, but saved Noah the eighth person, a preacher of righteousness, bringing in the flood upon the world of the ungodly" (2 Peter 2:5)

The ungodly sinners who reject Jesus will, no doubt, be judged at the 'Great White Thorne' and will be cast into the 'lake of fire' along with devil and his angels, and death and hell.

The godly are warned not to have company with ungodly. The godly are like the tree planted by the rivers of water and they delight in the word of God. The ungodly are like chaff which will be driven away by the wind.

The Lord knows the ways of the righteous but the ways of the ungodly shall perish. There is, however, hope for the ungodly sinners to seek help from the living God.

The word of God says all have sinned and come short of the glory of God and the wages of sin is death, but the gift of God, that is salvation, is free gift from God and it is eternal life through Jesus Christ our Lord.

 We are justified by his grace through redemption that is in Christ Jesus. For all those who accept Jesus Christ as their personal savior there is salvation and eternal life.

"For all have sinned, and come short of the glory of God; Being justified freely by his grace through the redemption that is in Christ Jesus" (Romans 3:23-24)

"For the wages of sin is death; but the gift of God is eternal life through Jesus Christ our Lord" (Romans 6:23)

DECEMBER DEVOTIONALS

DAY 1 LITTLE LOWER THAN ANGELS

Once I was watching a squirrel hop jump and move forward and then it turning back to see as if it missed something and later again hopping and jumping and moving in opposite direction.

My thoughts went back to ponder on the creation account mentioned in Genesis Chapter 1. God made heavens, earth, plants, and animals by His word and command, but when it came to make man God took some time to make him in his own image.

I was thinking that God may have taken quite a great deal of delight to see tiny flies move around, tiny birds jump around, animals jump around, lions roaring, and elephants moving around.

After creating man God desired to have fellowship with him and loved him so much. He gave him a helpmate and the man called her as Woman. The Woman was called as "Eve" because she was the mother of all living. The man was called as "Adam" (Gen. 2:19). The Woman was called as "Eve" (Gen 3:20).

When we create some art-work or draw a picture we are delighted to see our work and appreciate it. We want others to appreciate our work and appreciate us for doing that work. Let us think how much God desires to see we appreciate his work, his wisdom, and his ability to create the universe, the earth, the galaxy, the seas, you and me.

God also created supernatural heavenly beings that are called as Angels. The word in Hebrew and Greek from which the word "Angels" derived was also applied to human messengers.

It is recorded in Colossians 1:16 that all things whether visible or invisible were created by God and for him. In Hebrews 1:4-8 it is recorded that the Son of God, Lord Jesus Christ was greater than angels.

The Father said "Thou art my Son, this day I have begotten thee" and He has ordered the entire angelic host to worship the Son of God. The Father also said to him that his throne is for and ever and the scepter of righteousness is the scepter of his kingdom.

Yet when Jesus was in the form of man on this earth he was considered as little lower than the angels, just as man was considered as lower than the angels. Man is given the glory and honor to have dominion over all the works of God.

 The angels are the ministering spirits created by God. He takes care of the children of God. Jesus is always with the saved ones, and many times the children of God see angels helping children of God. Think about the wonderful way God has exalted man.

The words of Psalmist as prophesied in Psalm 8:3-9 are repeated in Hebrews 2:6-8 as fulfillment of the prophesy.

"When I consider thy heavens, the work of thy fingers, the moon and the stars, which thou hast ordained; What is man, that thou art mindful of him? and the son of man, that thou visitest him? For thou hast made him a little lower than the angels, and hast crowned him with glory and honour. Thou madest him to have dominion over the works of thy hands; thou hast put all things under his feet: All sheep and oxen, yea, and the beasts of the field" (Psalms 8:3-7)

And, in Hebrews 2:9 we have wonderful declaration that Jesus was made little lower than angels for suffering death on behalf of us and was crowned with glory and honor.

But we see Jesus, who was made a little lower than the angels for the suffering of death, crowned with glory and honour; that he by the grace of God should taste death for every man. (Hebrews 2:9)

DAY 2 LIVING IN HOPE

"Now the God of hope fill you with all joy and peace in believing, that ye may abound in hope, through the power of the Holy Ghost". Romans 15:13

Abraham was too old to have a son and Sarah his wife almost did not believe that she could have a child in her old age, yet both of them hoped in God's Word and believed on the promise God gave them that they will have a child and the seed of Abraham will be blessed to the extent that his descendants will be like stars in the sky and sand on the shore.

In the land of Egypt the children of Israel grew in number that posed a threat to the king of Egypt, who had already forgotten, who Joseph was. The birth of children in large numbers, from the Patriarchs, in the land of Egypt, caused fear in the mind of Pharaoh, who, therefore, ordered that every male child born to Israelites be killed.

Moses was born at a time when the children of his age were ordered to be killed by Pharaoh, yet the mother of Moses had faith and hope in God so she made a small basket of papyrus wood and lay her child in that basket, which she gently placed on the banks of Nile river.

The king appointed two Hebrew midwives, namely, "Shiphrah", and "Puah". (Exodus 1:15).

These midwives are ordered to kill every male baby that takes birth to Israelites, and concede female babies to live. This was the strategy of the king of Egypt, who hoped that such plan would eventually pave the way for diminishing number of male children in the houses of Israel, while the number of Egyptians would increase. However, the midwives did not obey the king of Egypt, because they feared God.

When the king of Egypt came to know about this, he called for these two Hebrew midwives and asked them why they did so. The midwives replied that the children were born even before they attempted to kill them, and thus, they escaped from the wrath of the king.

In the meanwhile, a man from the tribe of 'Levi' married a woman from the same tribe and had a son. When the woman saw that the child was exceedingly good, she hid him three months. (Acts 7:20 reads "In which time Moses was born, and was exceeding fair, and nourished up in his father's house three months").

Look at the providence and protection of God, who kept the child safe from all the dangerous living beings like sharks, or snakes or great fish.

The child was saved from the peril of the death. Not only was the child saved from the death, but Pharaoh's own daughter, who went down to the banks of Nile River to take bath found the baby lying in the basket and took it lovingly and adopted the child.

Look at the marvelous ways God works in the lives of His children. The child later grew and became the leader of Israelites. God fed his child with the provisions of his enemies!

Is there anything impossible with God? No. If God wants to help a person, no one can stand in the way of God's ways of executing His plans.

"And he said, The things which are impossible with men are possible with God". Luke 18:27

DAY 3 MEPHIBOSHETH

This devotional is from II Samuel 9th chapter

Two Kings in contrast in Old Testament were those who very often we speak of. One was King Saul and another King David. King Saul was rejected by God, while King David was accepted by God. King Saul sought after the life of David. Saul's daughter was David's wife, yet Saul was after the life of David.

Jonathan was the son of Saul. Jonathan was not only a close relative of David, but was his good friend. Jonathan's son was Mephibosheth.

Mephibosheth was very unfortunate in his life, because when he was just a child of five years, his nurse dropped him off her hands, and he became crippled and lame in his both legs.

Jonathan knew that David was chosen one of God and, therefore, requested David, to have mercy on his family. David was extremely kind to Saul's family even though Saul sought after his soul very often.

David asked Mephibosheth if there was anyone left in the family of Saul, that he could show mercy. Mephibosheth compared himself to a dead dog and inquired David, why he wanted to show kindness.

The word,"Dog" is a repulsive and most detested one used in the Bible. Mephibosheth compared himself as not only a dog but dead one.

We see David's kindness was so great that he not only gave Mephibosheth, his inheritance, but also granted him the privilege to dine with him, on his table, along with him, throughout his life.

But God, who is rich in mercy, for his great love wherewith he loved us, Even when we were dead in sins, hath quickened us together with Christ, (by grace ye are saved;) (Ephesians 2:4-5)

And if children, then heirs; heirs of God, and joint-heirs with Christ; if so be that we suffer with him, that we may be also glorified together. (Romans 8:17)

In Jesus Christ we see a greater love than this. He offered his own life for our sake and granted us salvation free of cost. He says, "Behold I stand at the door and knock. If anyone hears My voice and opens the door, I will come in to him and dine with him, and he with Me." (Revelation 3:20).

Lord Jesus Christ also said, "I am the living bread which came down from heaven. If anyone eats this bread, he will live for ever; and the bread that I shall give is My flesh, which I gave for the life of the world." (John 6:51)

Mephibosheth received inheritance and a place at the king David's table. Jesus calls us to receive our inheritance and have eternal life. Is there still anyone, who reads this message in need of the favor of Jesus Christ? Salvation is free of cost. Jesus paid the price for our sins. We only need to ask him forgiveness and accept Him as personal savior.

DAY 4 MILLENNIUM

THOUSAND YEAR REIGN OF LORD JESUS CHRIST

"And I saw an angel come down from heaven, having the key of the bottomless pit and a great chain in his hand". Revelation 20:1

John saw in his vision an angel coming down from heaven holding the key of the abyss and a huge chain in his hand. One fact that is very much noticeable here is that the angel coming down is not named. The angel is neither Michael nor Gabriel.

Satan is too inferior to the Father or the Son that the named powerful and mighty angels are not required to defeat him. It is enough that an unnamed angel is enough to bind Satan.

The Old Dragon, Satan, was already defeated at the cross and yet God has allowed him to be in the world with his limited power. Satan cannot do anything to any believer in Christ provided the believer depends on Lord Jesus Christ and has Him as rock of refuge. Otherwise, it will be like hitting hard a rock with a feeble fist.

The angel conquers Satan that cheated Eve and binds him and casts him into the abyss and shuts him up for thousand years in order that he may not deceive anyone and then he puts a seal on the bottom-less pit where Satan will be bound. Satan will be let loose for a short period of time after the thousand-year-rule by Jesus Christ is completed.

Then John saw that there were thrones and judgment was given unto those who sat upon them. He saw the souls of martyrs of those who stood for Jesus and for the word of God. He also saw those who did not worship Antichrist, or his image, or received the mark of the beast either on their hands or on their foreheads. They all lived and reigned with Christ for thousand years.

"And I saw thrones, and they sat upon them, and judgment was given unto them: and [I saw] the souls of them that were beheaded for the witness of Jesus, and for the word of God, and which had not worshipped the beast, neither his image, neither had received [his] mark upon their foreheads, or in their hands; and they lived and reigned with Christ a thousand years. But the rest of the dead lived not again until the thousand years were finished. This [is] the first resurrection" Revelation 20:4-5

These are those who faced Great Tribulation under Antichrist and successfully come out from his atrocious rule. Antichrist promises peace for seven years but after three and half years he breaks covenant and there will be great tribulation.

Jews will be cheated by his false promises. After facing Great Tribulation the Jews will call upon Jesus to save them and they will accept Jesus as their Messiah. They live and reign with Christ for thousand years.

This is the period when Jesus rules literally from the throne of David from Jerusalem and there would be peace everywhere. Satan will not be active at that period of time.

During the period of Antichrist the Jews face tremendous torture that surpasses any kind of tribulation, harassment, or torture faced by any body in the world from the beginning. The Jews need help during this time.

They are the 'brethren' of our Lord Jesus Christ who was himself a Jew. There are three classes mentioned in Matthew Chapter 25. They are the 'Sheep', the 'Goats' and the 'brethren'.

To the category of the Sheep belong those who help during the Great Tribulation period the 'brethren' of Jesus Christ and to the category of the Goats belong those who have neglected Jews during the Great Tribulation period.

When Jesus descends from the mid-air after the completion of seven-year period of Antichrist's rule, he steps on the Mount of Olives which is before Jerusalem.

The Mount of Olives cleaves in the midst towards the east and the west, resulting in a very great valley. Half of the mountain shall be removed toward the north and half toward the south. (Zechariah 14:4). This Valley is called 'Valley of Jehoshaphat'. (Joel 3:1-2)

There was no such place as 'Valley of Jehoshaphat' before or now is in Israel, but there will be such place in the future. The word 'Jehoshaphat' means 'The Lord Judges'. This is the throne of Jesus from where he judges the nations on this earth. Here he will gather all the nations to judge.

Those whom Jesus justifies as having helped his 'brethren' and those Jews who have accept Jesus as Messiah during Great Tribulation period will enter into literal thousand year reign by Lord Jesus Christ. Jesus says to the nations who have helped the 'brethren' "Verily I say unto you, Inasmuch as ye have done it unto one of the least of these my brethren, ye have done it unto me".

Those whom Jesus does not justify as having helped the 'brethren' during Great Tribulation will not be in the thousand year rule by Jesus Christ, but will be cast out. Jesus says to them 'Depart from me, ye cursed, into everlasting fire, prepared for the devil and his angels'.

We who are in the Church saved by the grace of God, having been washed in the blood of Jesus Christ will be with Him for ever and ever in bodies that are transformed in a twinkling of an eye at the last trump (Ref. 1 Corinthians 15:52). This happens when the trumpet sounds when the Lord himself shall descend from heaven as recorded in 1 Thessalonians 4:16-17

DAY 5 NO ONE IS PERFECT

"And be found in him, not having mine own righteousness, which is of the law, but that which is through the faith of Christ, the righteousness which is of God by faith" (Philippians 3:9)

A person's efforts to gain salvation and imputation of righteousness by good works and by being obedient to the Old Testament laws and commandments would be futile. Failure to keep one law is tantamount to breaking all the laws.

The law points guilt of a person and never saves him. It is the blood of Lord Jesus Christ alone that cleanses a sinner of his/her sins.

Apostle Paul repeatedly wrote this fact in his epistles. He was happy that the righteousness that was imputed to him was not through the good works that he did, but through the faith in Jesus Christ.

He was happy that the Old Testament law did not provide him the blessedness of being called as righteous. Also, his own good works could not provide him salvation. He was happy to know the truth that he was righteous because it was bestowed on him though faith in God. He was also happy to know the fact about his resurrection.

In the epistle to Philippians 3:13-14 Paul says that he does not want to count himself as having become perfect. He realizes that the purpose of his calling to serve Lord Jesus Christ was not fulfilled.

There was always something short of expectation in him, and the need was always there to go beyond what he has already achieved. There was always still some area where he needed to be perfect. His message to us is clear that it is not possible for any man to become perfect, but his message is that one can do one's best to become perfect.

It was just as he himself failed in his ventures, and, therefore, he desires that everyone would press on further, just as he would do, to achieve goals to please God who called him through Lord Jesus Christ.

It is, therefore, apt for every child of God not to grumble when he/she faces any suffering, but rejoice in God because every child of God will be heir of God and joint-heir with Lord Jesus Christ.

Paul said that he did not reckon his sufferings could be compared with the abundant blessings he would receive in eternity. He goes on to give us the blessed hope that our sufferings are not so intense when they are to stand in comparison with the glory that would be revealed to us.(Romans 8:17-18)

"I press toward the mark for the prize of the high calling of God in Christ Jesus" (Philippians 3:14)

DAY 6 PETER AND JOHN TESTIFY

Peter and John who saw Jesus testified about him

While he yet spake, behold, a bright cloud overshadowed them: and behold a voice out of the cloud, which said, This is my beloved Son, in whom I am well pleased; hear ye him. (Matthew 17:5)

Peter and also the two sons of Zebedee (James and John) saw Jesus transfigured and his face shone as the sun, and his raiment was white as light, when he appeared to them. They also heard the Father saying"... This is my beloved Son, in whom I am well pleased; hear ye him..." (Matthew 17:5).

Peter was perturbed on hearing false stories about Jesus and about the unbelief about Jesus. Therefore, he testified that he and James and John witnessed the event of transfiguration of Jesus. Peter said that they did not follow cunning devised fables about Jesus; but they made known about Jesus and his glory to them as eye witnesses. Peter testified that they made known unto them the power and coming of Lord Jesus Christ.

They said that they were eye witnesses of his majesty and that they heard the voice that came down from heaven, while they were on the holy mountain. (2 Peter 1:16-18) Peter heard Jesus say that the Father loves him because he lays down his life and will take it again. (John 10:17).

John testified that "the Word was made flesh, and dwelt among us, (and we beheld his glory, the glory as of the only begotten of the Father,) full of grace and truth". (John 1:14)

True, we enjoy the benefits of the love of God because Jesus laid down his life our sake; "But God raised him from the dead" (Acts 13:30). We are cleansed of our sins by the blood of Jesus Christ shed on the cross. This is the truth and faith in him alone saves a person from damnation.

Do not trust every spirit, but test the sprits to know for yourself whether or not those spirits are of God. There are many false prophets and preachers gone out into this world.

The way to know whether someone is from the living God or not is to make sure whether or not that person confesses that Jesus Christ is the incarnation of the Father and dwelt among us. Anyone, who does not confess that Jesus is come in the flesh, is not of God but of antichrist.

There are many out there now who say that a man can gain salvation by good works. It is time we know them and realize that they are not from God.

If you are not yet saved, here is word from Apostle Paul, who says that if you confess with your mouth the Lord Jesus and believe in your heart that God raised him from the dead you shall be saved. (Romans 10:9)

DAY 7 PRIDE GOES BEFORE FALL

David and Goliath

"And when the Philistine looked about, and saw David, he despised him: for he was but a youth, and ruddy, and of a fair countenance. And the Philistine said unto David, Am I a dog that you come to me with sticks? And the Philistine cursed David by his gods. (1 Samuel" 17:42-43)

Philistine warrior Goliath depended on his height, might, and strength, while David depended on the mightiest of mighty. "Is there anyone to challenge me?" shouted the Philistine giant, Goliath, for forty days at the children of God, the Israelites.

None of the children of Jesse or any one of the Israelites in the camp dared to go out and face the nine feet tall giant, who wore protective dress weighing 150 shekels. Goliath boasted and hurled insults at God's children saying, I am a Philistine, and you are servants to Saul.

"Then said David to the Philistine, You come to me with a sword, and with a spear, and with a shield: but I come to you in the name of the LORD of hosts, the God of the armies of Israel, whom you have defied. This day will the LORD deliver you into my hand; and I will strike you, and take your head from you; and I will give the carcases of the host of the Philistines this day unto the fowls of the air, and to the wild beasts of the earth; that all the earth may know that there is a God in Israel." (1 Samuel 17:45, 46)

Look at the faith and confidence the child of God had. He had his hope in the everlasting God; the mightiest of all; the Lord of hosts. Goliath arose, went to meet David in the battlefield, and drew close, like a stalking mountain, overlaid with brass and iron.

David advanced with greater strength in God and cheerfulness, as one that aimed more to execute God's command rather than to make a figure of himself. David, who was lightly clad hasted, and ran to meet the Philistine. Before honor is humility.

"And he took his staff in his hand, and chose him five smooth stones out of the brook, and put them in a shepherd's bag which he had, even in a pouch; and his sling was in his hand: and he drew near to the Philistine". (1 Samuel 17:40)

David put one of the five pebbles in the sling and hurled at Goliath. There it was! The pebble struck straight at Goliath's forehead and in the twinkling of an eye, it fetched him to the ground. Goliath fell with his face down on the ground.

See how frail and uncertain the life is. Even when we think it is best fortified how quickly, how easily, and with how small a matter, there would be a passage that opens the door for life to exit and death to enter.

Pride goes before fall while before honor is humility. Did David need his own sword to kill his enemy? No! His enemy's sword served his purpose. God is greatly glorified when his proud enemies are cut off with their own sword and he makes their own tongues to fall upon them David rushed forward pulled out the sword of Goliath and killed him.

David used Goliath's own weapon to kill him. God was with David. Goliath's strength and power were of no avail before God's strength and power.

The same God, the living Lord, who has sent His Son, Jesus Christ, into this world for the remission of your sins and mine, calls you now, as "my son/daughter, Depend on me. I am your Savior. I want to be your rock of refuge and bless you."

DAY 8 PUBLIC MINISTRY OF JESUS

"This beginning of miracles did Jesus in Cana of Galilee, and manifested forth his glory; and his disciples believed on him". John 2:11

Jesus started his ministry with the miracle that he did in Cana of Galilee, where he manifested forth his glory in order that his disciples and others there would believe that he was the Messiah. Jesus came into this world relinquishing the glory that he had with the Father and took the form of man.

While on this world he lived like an ordinary man, yet with full divine power. He did miracles that were unknown to the natives of Galilee, Nazareth, Capernaum and the surrounding areas. Very few miracles are only recorded in the Scriptures.

Jesus did many miracles according to John 21:25 but very few are recorded that are sufficient for unbelievers to know about his power and glory that he had with the Father. In the miracle that Jesus did at Cana, where he turned water into wine, he manifested forth his glory. For the disciples, whom he called from the general and poor folk, to follow him, this miracle was a great consolation and rest on him in faith that he was the true Messiah.

They believed on him. Jesus was walking by the Sea of Galilee, where he saw two brothers; Simon called Peter and Andrew his brother, who were casting a net into the sea to catch fishes.

Jesus asked them to follow him promising that he would make them fishers of men. (Matthew 4:18-20).

They immediately left their nets and followed him. This miracle that Jesus did at Cana was the first one in his ministry when he was about thirty years of age.

Dear Friend,

Believe in Jesus that you may have eternal life.

"Verily, verily, I say unto you, He that heareth my word, and believeth on him that sent me, hath everlasting life, and shall not come into condemnation; but is passed from death unto life". John 5:24

DAY 9 PUT ON THE ARMOUR OF GOD

"Put on the whole armour of God, that ye may be able to stand against the wiles of the devil". (Ephesians 6:11)

In the battle that was to take place between the army of Philistines and the army of children of Israel both were advantageously posted, yet neither went forward to fight against each other. Philistine hero Goliath was waiting for an equivalent opponent.

Saul thought there was none on his side to fight against this mighty proud warrior. David the youngest son of Jesse, looking after his father's sheep, went to watch as to what was happening in the battlefield. To his surprise, he found that none from the Israelites' camp went forward to fight against Goliath.

Deeply distressed over the attitude of his brothers and also that of others in the camp, he agreed to fight with Goliath. He retorted saying, "Who is this uncircumcised fellow to mock at God's children?" David took the challenge and went forward to face Goliath.

Seeing the shepherd boy the giant Goliath insulted him. David was a shepherd boy, short in stature and did not attire himself in good dress. Saul was worried about the intervention of this shepherd boy, David. "And Saul said to David, Thou art not able to go against this Philistine to fight with him: for thou art but a youth, and he a man of war from his youth". (1 Samuel 17:33)

What a discouragement David had to face from Saul! Yet after hearing David's courageous acts Saul conceded to David to fight against the Philistine but asked David to wear "his armour, and he put on helmet of brass upon his head and also armed him with a coat of mail". (1 Samuel 17:38).

Saul thought armor, helmet of brass and coat are required to meet challenge of enemy. He insisted upon David to wear armor of his choice to face Goliath.

Saul himself did not have courage to face Goliath but he thought David needed his choice armor to face the enemy. David girded his sword upon his armour and found uncomfortable. He removed it saying that he can not go with the armour that Saul has provided him. (1 Samuel 17:39)

David took his staff and chose five smooth stones out of the brook and he slang a stone from his sling. The stone sunk into Goliath's forehead and he fell upon his face to the earth. (1 Samuel 17:40 and 49)

David ran and stood upon Philistine and took his sword and killed him and the philistines fled from the battlefield (1 Samuel 17:50-51)

David used Goliath's own weapon to kill him. God was with David. Goliath's strength and power were of no avail before God's.

The same God, the living Lord, who has sent His Son, Jesus Christ, into this world for the remission of your sins and mine, calls us to depend on Him because He is our savior.

He wants to be our rock of refuge and bless us. He wants us to put on the armour that he gave us instead of putting on the armour that the world gives us. Let not the strong man glory in his strength.

DAY 10 TAKE REFUGE IN THE LIVING GOD

This meditation is about two individuals in the war between Philistines and the children of Israel at a land that belonged to Judah. The first one was Goliath, who was proud, huge, tall, strong man from Philistines. The second one was David, the son of Jesse, who belonged to the children of Israel.

Philistines took pride in their leader Goliath in the battle at Shochloh, which beloged to Judah. Saul and men of Israel gathered on the other side by the valley of Elah. Philistines stood on a mountain on one side and the Israel stood on a mountain on the other side (1 Samuel 17:1-3)

Saul was the first king of Israel. He was the son of Kish from the tribe of Benjamin. He was young, handsome and taller than anyone among the children of Israel. (1 Samuel 9:1-2)

There was no response to Goliath's challenge either from Saul or anyone from Israel until the ruddy shepherd David came along to take up the challenge.

Goliath looked upon David with scorn and shouted. Goliath ridiculed the God of Israel and wondered if David thought that Goliath was a dog! He boasted in his gods and said that he would give David's flesh to the fowls of the air and to the beasts of the field.

The response from David who hoped in the Almighty and living God was equally challenging. David honored the living God when he said to Goliath that he was facing the mighty man in the name of the Lord of hosts, the God of armies of Israel, whom Goliath defied.

"Then said David to the Philistine, Thou comest to me with a sword, and with a spear, and with a shield: but I come to thee in the name of the LORD of hosts, the God of the armies of Israel, whom thou hast defied.

This day will the LORD deliver thee into mine hand; and I will smite thee, and take thine head from thee; and I will give the carcases of the host of the Philistines this day unto the fowls of the air, and to the wild beasts of the earth; that all the earth may know that there is a God in Israel". (1 Samuel 17:45-46)

Goliath arose, went to meet David in the battlefield, and drew close, like a stalking mountain, overlaid with brass and iron.

 David advanced with greater strength in God and cheerfulness, as one that aimed more to execute God's command rather than to make a figure: He hasted, and ran, was being lightly clad, to meet the Philistine. Before honor is humility.

David put one of the pebbles in the sling and hurled at Goliath. There it was! The pebble struck straight at Goliath's forehead and in the twinkling of an eye, it fetched him to the ground. Goliath fell with his face down on the ground.

"Therefore David ran, and stood upon the Philistine, and took his sword, and drew it out of the sheath thereof, and slew him, and cut off his head therewith. And when the Philistines saw their champion was dead, they fled". (1 Samuel 17:51)

DAY 11 BELIEVE IN THE POWER OF THE LORD

"And the LORD said unto him, Who hath made man's mouth? or who maketh the dumb, or deaf, or the seeing, or the blind? have not I the LORD?" (Exodus 4:11)

When God chose Moses to be the leader to lead the children of Israel from Egypt unto the Promised Land Canaan, the land flowing with milk and honey Moses was very reluctant to take the lead. Moses speaks to God in a very negative way when he says…

"…But, behold, they will not believe me, nor hearken unto my voice: for they will say, The LORD hath not appeared unto thee…" Exodus 4:1

This is how we Christians sometimes make decisions on our own in unbelief, or reluctance or fear saying, "Oh! God that is not possible; they may not hear me; they may not entertain me; they may not believe what I say about you" and so on.

God showed to Moses that He was Almighty One, and asked him as to what in his hand was. Moses answered and said 'a rod'. God asks him to cast that rod on the ground. Moses obeys and casts it on the ground.

To the surprise of Moses the rod became serpent and he tried to flee from the scene, but then upon God's intervention Moses went back and caught the serpent by its tail as commanded by God and the serpent turned rod.

Next, God said to Moses to draw his hand in to his bosom and pull it out to see the result. Moses does it as God said to him, and finds the color of the skin on his hand turning out to be like one of leper's hand. On God's instructions when he draws his hand back again into the bosom and pulls it out he sees the hand has its natural color.

God now tells Moses that in spite of showing these miracles if the Israelites do not believe that Moses is the chosen one to be their leader he should take water from the river and pour it on the ground; the water then would become blood upon the dry land.

It would seem that Moses was an unbelieving man in the light of his refusals to believe that the miracles shown to him were not sufficient, but went on giving excuses to God saying "...LORD, O my Lord, I am not eloquent, neither heretofore, nor since thou hast spoken unto thy servant: but I am slow of speech, and of a slow tongue". Exodus 4:10

After hearing the excuses of Moses, the LORD said unto him:

"...Who hath made man's mouth? or who maketh the dumb, or deaf, or the seeing, or the blind? have not I the LORD?" Exodus 4:11

God said to Moses very firmly that he should go and lead Israelites by instilling sufficient confidence in Moses saying God himself would be his mouth, and would teach him what he needs to do. Moses obeyed after much reluctance and God was with him.

Believe that God does miracles. In just two verses of Matthew 9:28-29 it can be seen that those two blind men who believed were saved and they received sight.

"And when he was come into the house, the blind men came to him: and Jesus saith unto them, Believe ye that I am able to do this? They said unto him, Yea, Lord. Then touched he their eyes, saying, According to your faith be it unto you" (Matthew 9:28-29)

DAY 12 ALMIGHTY GOD IS OUR STRENGTH

When the LORD God is our strength who can be against us?

Even when Moses was in low spirits with his reluctant responses given to the Almighty God that he is not fit to lead the children of Israel out from the bondage of slavery the LORD God infuses courage and confidence in the mind of Moses. The LORD says to Moses that He made Moses a god to pharaoh. Pause for a while and think about the word 'god'. God says He made Moses a 'god' to Pharaoh.

Hebrew word that was used in this context gives us the meaning that God made Moses a judge over Pharaoh, who was the king of Egypt. Pharaoh, who had all the authority in the land of Egypt became at the word of God a subservient to Moses, who was not a king, nor was a strong man to be able to fight with Pharaoh, yet the Almighty God said to him that He made Moses a 'god' to Pharaoh. God assured that Aaron, the brother of Moses will be his prophet.

The power of the LORD is exhibited before Pharaoh when Aaron spoke at the command of the LORD to send the children of Israel out of his hand. The LORD's desire was to show His strength by which He delivered the children of Israel from the bondage of slavery. Until then Pharaoh hardened his heart partly at the making of the LORD and partly in his arrogance by his own making.

The LORD could have secured the redemption of Israel in a very easy way; after all Pharaoh was a human being but the LORD desired to show His signs and His wonders in the land of Egypt.

Until then Pharaoh's heart remained hardened. Even though Pharaoh saw the signs and wonders from the LORD, he hesitated to release the children of Israel. Pharaoh did not yield fully until the LORD killed the firstborn of Pharaoh. The LORD could have killed Pharaoh instantly or gradually but the LORD wanted him to realize the pain of losing his firstborn.

The LORD showed the Egyptians that He is the Almighty God by laying His heavy hand and outstretched arm and by great judgments upon them.

Apostle Paul brings home the point to our edification and reliance on the LORD by saying who could be against us if God is with us. The LORD God having not spared His own Son but gave Him for our sake, how would He not give all good things feely for us? Who could lay charge against us when the LORD has justified of not guilty of sin? Christ died and rose from the dead and He is alive today.

"What shall we then say to these things? If God [be] for us, who [can be] against us? He that spared not his own Son, but delivered him up for us all, how shall he not with him also freely give us all things? Who shall lay any thing to the charge of God's elect? [It is] God that justifieth. Who [is] he that condemneth? [It is] Christ that died, yea rather, that is risen again, who is even at the right hand of God, who also maketh intercession for us. Who shall separate us from the love of Christ? [shall] tribulation, or distress, or persecution, or famine, or nakedness, or peril, or sword?" Romans 8:31-35

DAY 13 MOSES AND AARON STRENGTHENED

Moses is strengthened in his confidence and reliance on the LORD and goes along with Aaron his brother to demand the release of the children of Israel. Moses realized that if it is not for the help of the LORD Almighty it was impossible to secure their redemption.

They had to establish, firstly, before the children of Israel that they were chosen by the LORD and were authorized leaders separated for the purpose by the LORD God. Secondly, they had to present themselves before Pharaoh with authority and demand the release of the children of Israel from the bondage as desired by the LORD.

Pharaoh would not let them go and His heart was hardened time and again. He would say that they may go but not long before they start going he would refuse to release them. Pharaoh showed his refusal or trickery or arrogance not once but ten times until his firstborn and the firstborn in the land of Egypt, except of the children of Israel were killed.

In all the occasions when plagues were brought upon the land of Egypt the children of Israel and the area where they lived was secure and protected by the LORD God of Israel. It was by the miracle of turning the Aarons' rod that they try to establish their authority to demand the redemption of the children of Israel.

It was Aaron who threw the rod on the ground contrary to some mistakes inadvertently made by some that Moses threw his rod on the ground; not so. At the instruction of Moses Aaron threw his rod on the ground and the rod turned a serpent. But then, the magicians in Egypt also threw their rods on the ground at the behest of Pharaoh and showed the miracle.

However, Aaron' rod that turned into serpent swallowed the serpents of the magicians thus showing the supremacy of the LORD. (Ref. Exodus 7:8-9)

It is worth remembering the ten plagues. Many of us so involved in learning New Testament Truths and do not remember the Old Testament Truths. The New Testament truths cannot be understood well if our base is not good in the knowledge of the Old Testament.

The first two signs were not plagues but they were given to Moses and Aaron to prove that they are from the living God. Moses and Aaron showed only one sign and that is of the Aaron's rod that turned into serpent.

The Ten Plagues are:

1. Water turned in to blood 2. Frogs produced in the land of Egypt 3. Lice flew from the dust 4. Flies pestered Egyptians 5. Murrain 6. Boils 7. Hails 8. Locusts 9. Darkness 10. First Born killed

When Lord Jesus healed one possessed with devil, and was blind and dumb Pharisees accused Lord Jesus Christ.

"Then was brought unto him one possessed with a devil,

blind, and dumb: and he healed him, insomuch that the blind and dumb both spake and saw. And all the people were amazed, and said, Is not this the son of David? But when the Pharisees heard it, they said, This fellow doth not cast out devils, but by Beelzebub the prince of the devils". (Matthew 12:22-24)

However, Jesus knowing their thoughts said to them.

"And if Satan cast out Satan, he is divided against himself; how shall then his kingdom stand?" Matthew 12:26

Although Moses and Aaron were not accused with such profane words, yet it is but natural that such thoughts rise in the minds of some people on seeing miracles from God.

No wonder, Pharaoh's heart was hardened because his magicians could do the same thing that Moses and Aaron could do. However, the serpents of Pharaoh's magicians were swallowed by the Aaron's rod that turned as serpent.

DAY 14 PRIDE GOES BEFORE FALL

"And when the Philistine looked about, and saw David, he despised him: for he was but a youth, and ruddy, and of a fair countenance. And the Philistine said unto David, Am I a dog that you come to me with sticks? And the Philistine cursed David by his gods. (1 Samuel" 17:42-43)

Philistine warrior Goliath depended on his height, might, and strength, while David depended on the mightiest of mighty. "Is there any one to challenge me?" shouted the Philistine giant, Goliath, for forty days at the children of God, the Israelites.

None of the children of Jesse, or any one of the Israelites in the camp dared to go out and face the nine feet tall giant, who wore protective dress weighing 150 shekels. Goliath boasted and hurled insults at God's children saying, I am a Philistine, and you are servants to Saul.

"Then said David to the Philistine, You come to me with a sword, and with a spear, and with a shield: but I come to you in the name of the LORD of hosts, the God of the armies of Israel, whom you have defied. This day will the LORD deliver you into my hand; and I will strike you, and take your head from you; and I will give the carcases of the host of the Philistines this day unto the fowls of the air, and to the wild beasts of the earth; that all the earth may know that there is a God in Israel." (1 Samuel 17:45, 46)

Look at the faith and confidence the child of God had. He had his hope in the everlasting God; the mightiest of all; the Lord of hosts. Goliath arose, went to meet David in the battlefield, and drew close, like a stalking mountain, overlaid with brass and iron.

David advanced with greater strength in God and cheerfulness, as one that aimed more to execute God's command rather than to make a figure: He hasted, and ran, was being lightly clad, to meet the Philistine. Before honor is humility.

"And he took his staff in his hand, and chose him five smooth stones out of the brook, and put them in a shepherd's bag which he had, even in a pouch; and his sling was in his hand: and he drew near to the Philistine". (1 Samuel 17:40)

David put one of the five pebbles in the sling and hurled at Goliath. There it was! The pebble struck straight at Goliath's forehead and in the twinkling of an eye, it fetched him to the ground. Goliath fell with his face down on the ground.

See how frail and uncertain the life is. Even when we think it is best fortified how quickly, how easily, and with how small a matter, there would be a passage that opens the door for life to exit and death to enter. Pride goes before fall while before honor is humility.

Did David need his own sword to kill his enemy? No! His enemy's sword served his purpose. God is greatly glorified when his proud enemies are cut off with their own swords and he makes their own tongues to fall upon them.

David rushed forward pulled out the sword of Goliath and killed him. David used Goliath's own weapon to kill him. God was with David. Goliath's strength and power were of no avail before God's strength and power.

The same God, the living Lord, who has sent His only begotten Son, Jesus Christ, into this world for the remission of your sins and mine, calls you now, as "my son/my daughter, depend on me. I am your Savior. I want to be your rock of refuge and bless you." Let not the strong man glory in his strength.

DAY 15 RIVER WATER TURNED INTO BLOOD

"And Moses and Aaron did so, as the LORD commanded; and he lifted up the rod, and smote the waters that were in the river, in the sight of Pharaoh, and in the sight of his servants; and all the waters that were in the river were turned to blood. And the fish that was in the river died; and the river stank, and the Egyptians could not drink of the water of the river; and there was blood throughout all the land of Egypt" (Exodus 7:20-21)

Egyptians considered the fertility around River Nile as from their god and, therefore, they idolized the river and worshipped it. The Nile River was a national pride of Egyptians and the water from that river was like fine beverage for them and in addition fish in the river was fine food for them.

God hates Idolatry and idols to the extreme and He is against every individual and every nation who gives pre-eminence to the idols in their lives. The very first commandment God gave after the redemption of children of Israel was that they shall not have other gods before Him (Ref. Exodus 20:3).

God will not give His glory to anyone or to any graven image. God would not hesitate to remove the object of our worship from our lives if it is not Him. In all things God of Heavens, the God of Abraham, the God of Isaac, the God of Jacob, the Father of our Lord Jesus Christ should receive our worship and He should be pre-eminent in our lives.

"I am the LORD: that is my name: and my glory will I not give to another, neither my praise to graven images" (Isaiah 42:8)

When Pharaoh refused to let the children of Israel go at the first demand made by Moses God commanded Moses to go the river brink and wait for Pharaoh who would come there for washing himself in the morning.

This would be the time when Moses and Aaron would demand letting the people of Israel go and worship their God and if Pharaoh refused to let them go, God would smite the water and turn it into blood. God said that He would turn not only the water in the river in to blood but also cause fish in the river to die and river to stink that the Egyptians would loathe to drink the water from the river.

God told Moses to speak unto Aaron to stretch his rod "...upon the waters of Egypt, upon their streams, upon their rivers, and upon their ponds, and upon all their pools of water, that they may become blood; and that there may be blood throughout all the land of Egypt, both in vessels of wood, and in vessels of stone". Exodus 7:19

Moses and Aaron obeyed as God commanded them to do and Aaron lifted up his rod and smote the river water in the presence of Pharaoh and the fish in the river died and river stank. Egyptians dug the earth but did not find water anywhere in the land of Egypt and the plague lasted for seven days.

The plague hit not only the Nile River but also the pools, ponds and canals. The magicians of Pharaoh also did the same and the water turned into blood and that made Pharaoh to harden his heart again but then Magicians had no power reverse their magic in order to turn blood into water again.

God turned River Nile which Egyptian worshipped into blood as it was necessary at the point of time and turned blood into water again after seven days.

Lord Jesus Christ, Son of God, while speaking to Samaritan woman said that the water that He gives has everlasting life and no one would thirst again. If anyone drank water that Lord Jesus gives he would have everlasting life.

The first miracle Jesus died in His ministry on this earth was to turn water into wine at the marriage of Cana where there was shortage of wine and the help from Lord Jesus was most needed. (Ref. John 2:1). Believe in Lord Jesus Christ and receive everlasting life.

"But whosoever drinketh of the water that I shall give him shall never thirst; but the water that I shall give him shall be in him a well of water springing up into everlasting life"(John 4:14)

DAY 16 GOD'S ANGER OVER IDOL WORSHIPPERS

Ahaziah was son of Ahab (1 Kings 22:51). Ahaziah, who fell down from his upper chamber through the lattice and became sick. The king sent his messengers to Baalzebub, the god of Ekron to know if he would have recovery from the disease. (Baalzebub was believed to be a god of Philistines. He was believed to have given out oracles and protected them from flies, and therefore, he was also known as "the Lord of flies" [Ref. International Standard Bible Encyclopedia and Geneva Bible footnotes]). Ekron was one of the cities in the northern part of Israel. (Ref: Joshua 15:11; 1Samuel 5:10; 6:16-17).

Ahaziah hoped in a god made in the form of idol by man. He purposed to know if he would have recovery from the injuries and the disease that he suffered after his fall through the lattice from his upper chamber. As if the God of Israel, who redeemed them from the bondage of slavery under Pharaoh, was not strong enough, Ahaziah depended on some material that appeared like god.

God was very angry over Ahaziah's reliance on Baalzebub, an idol god at Ekron. The Angel of the Lord said to Elijah the Tishbite, to ask Ahaziah if his dependency on idol was because he thought there was no living God in Israel. Elijah met the messengers from Ahaziah on their way to Ekron, and said the words that the Angel of the Lord had put in his mouth.

The messengers returned to Ahaziah and Ahaziah asked them how the man who spoke those words looked like. The messengers described him as a man in a hairy garment, and girt with a girdle of leather. Ahaziah recognized that he was Elijah the Tishbite, who spoke those words and he sent to him a captain of fifty with his fifty. The captain of fifty with his fifty said to Elijah the Tishbite to go with them to the king. At Elijah's prayer the captain and the fifty were consumed.

Ahaziah sent another captain of fifty with his fifty. The captain said to Elijah to go to the king quickly. At Elijah's prayers the second captain and his fifty were also consumed. (Ref. 2 Kings 1:10-12)

Then, Ahaziah's third captain of fifty went to Elijah and fell on his knees before him and begged him to spare his life and the lives of his fifty men.

Fire came down from heaven and consumed the two former captains and their fifty men each, but this time, the Angel of the Lord said to Elijah not to be afraid but go with him. Elijah obeyed the word from the Angel of the Lord and stood before the king and asked him if it was because he thought that there was no living God in Israel that he sent his messengers to Baalzebub, the god of Ekron.

Elijah said to Ahaziah that because he believed and relied on the god made by man for his healing, instead of depending on the living God, he would not rise from his bed but die. According to the word of Jehovah that Elijah spoke to Ahaziah, the king Ahaziah died and his place was taken by Jehoram, the son of Jehoshaphat, king of Judah. (Ahaziah had no son)

Let us hope in the Living God, for all our needs, may they be sickness or any other need.

"For we are saved by hope: but hope that is seen is not hope: for what a man seeth, why doth he yet hope for? But if we hope for that we see not, then do we with patience wait for it". (Romans 8:24-25)

DAY 17 WAIT ON THE LORD

"Wait on the LORD, and keep his way, and he shall exalt thee to inherit the land: when the wicked are cut off, thou shalt see [it]. I have seen the wicked in great power, and spreading himself like a green bay tree. Yet he passed away, and, lo, he [was] not: yea, I sought him, but he could not be found. Mark the perfect [man], and behold the upright: for the end of [that] man [is] peace". Psalm 37:34-37

David fought many battles successfully and led his people to victory. He was a man of wars and tasted the love of God. Early in his life he defeated Philistine giant Goliath and was anointed as king over Israel. He worshipped the LORD with all his heart, with his entire mind and with all his soul.

David, having seen such great victories in his life advises to wait on the LORD and follow His ways. Even though he was anointed as King over Israel he waited for the LORD to dethrone King Saul before he occupied his throne as King (Ref. 1 Samuel 16:13)

When we exalt the name of the LORD He will exalt us in due time. David saw the wicked grow in power and spreading himself like a green bay tree, a tree that grows in its own soil but then, when he was gone, he was gone forever and could not be found. The perfect man has peace and is upright.

David saw the nature's beauty, the creation of God, took

care of his sheep, and saw the strength of the LORD in him when he killed the lion and the bear to protect his sheep. David had a great confidence in the LORD that He would help him in killing the uncircumcised Goliath. (Ref. 1 Samuel 17:36)

David spared the life of Saul who was pursuing him. Saul took three thousand chosen men out of Israel to seek David and kill him when he was told that David was in the wilderness of Engedi. David and his men were in the sides of the cave and when David saw that Saul was taking rest he went and cut a piece off the skirt of Saul's robe secretly.

David was remorseful for cutting a piece off the skirt of Saul and said to himself that the LORD may forbid him to do any harm to Saul, who was anointed one (Ref. 1 Samuel 10:1). Then David said to his men not to do any harm to Saul. David's purpose was only to show to Saul that he was not pursuing to kill Saul.

When Saul looked at David he stooped and bowed down to him and showed the piece of the skirt that he had cut off of the robe of Saul and asked him why he believed the words of people who said to him that he was pursuing Saul to kill him.

David made Saul realize that the LORD delivered him into his hands that night and if he desired he could have killed Saul in the cave. David said to Saul that some even asked him to kill Saul but he spared Saul's life. David went on saying that the LORD be judge between them.

Saul then understood David fully and blessed him saying the David was more righteous than himself. He sought to kill David but David spared the Saul's life. Humbling himself Saul said to David that he knew that one day David would be the King over Israel and, therefore, pleaded that David may spare the seed of Saul. David's goodness is seen in allowing Mephibosheth, a crippled grandson of Saul to dine with him on his table throughout his life during his reign as King over Israel. (Ref. 1 Samuel 24:1-22, and II Samuel 9).

Saul was rejected by God and he had his end. Saul did an abominable thing by seeking the witch at Endor to bring up Samuel's soul. Saul had his last word from Samuel that his kingdom was taken out his hand and given it to David. (1 Samuel 28:17-19).

"Then said Saul unto his armourbearer, Draw thy sword, and thrust me through therewith; lest these uncircumcised come and thrust me through, and abuse me. But his armourbearer would not; for he was sore afraid. Therefore Saul took a sword, and fell upon it". (1 Samuel 31:4)

There is a day for the wicked and they shall see their end. There is a day for the righteous and they shall see the glory of the Lord and be with Him for ever and ever.

"So shall it be at the end of the world: the angels shall come forth, and sever the wicked from among the just, And shall cast them into the furnace of fire: there shall be wailing and gnashing of teeth". (Matthew 13:49-50)

DAY 18 THE LORD GIVES DESIRE OF YOUR HEART

"Trust in the LORD, and do good; so shalt thou dwell in the land, and verily thou shalt be fed. Delight thyself also in the LORD; and he shall give thee the desires of thine heart. Commit thy way unto the LORD; trust also in him; and he shall bring it to pass. And he shall bring forth thy righteousness as the light, and thy judgment as the noonday" (Psalms 37:3-6)

David recalls the promise the LORD God of Israel made with his fathers that if they keep the statues and His commandments and obey them, then the LORD will shower upon them multiple blessings. As we read through the blessings we see that the blessings from the LORD are far greater than anyone would think of.

There is a condition attached to receiving these blessings and that is committing one's ways to the LORD and then He will fulfill one's heart's desires. His promises never fail and they are as true as the light of the day and His judgment is as true as the noonday. He promised to the people of Israel that He will give them…

Rain in due season: The Land shall yield her increase. Fruit: He will cause the trees to yield their fruit; their threshing shall reach unto the annual produce of the grape harvest, the vintage will reach unto sowing time and they shall eat their bread to the full.

Safety: They will live in their land safely.

Peace: They will have peace in the Land

Courage to be free from fear: They shall lie down and none shall make them afraid

Strength to chase out evil beasts: He will rid evil beasts out of the Land

The Sword: No sword will go through their Land – They shall be free from wars.

The Victory: Five of them will chase one hundred and hundred will chase ten thousand. Enemies will fall by their sword.

Respect: God will have respect unto them. He will make them fruitful, multiply them and establish covenant with them.

Abundance in food: They will eat from old store to make space for their new yield.

His presence: The LORD will set up His tabernacle among them. His soul will not abhor them and He will walk among them. He will be their God they shall be His people.

The LORD reminds them that He brought them out of the Land of Egypt and redeemed them from the bondage of slavery. They will walk upright with courage and confidence. (Ref. Leviticus 26:3-13). These blessings are reiterated elaborately again in Deuteronomy 28:1-4)

In Lord Jesus Christ we have all these blessings from the Father because we believe in Him. Earthly inheritance of the Promised Land foreshadowed the spiritual blessings that the children of God will inherit.

The inheritance of God is the soul's everlasting possession and those who have God as their portion in their lives will have the pleasure of God working in them insomuch that everything works for good for them on this earth (Ref. Romans 8:28)

"He that overcometh shall inherit all things; and I will be his God, and he shall be my son" (Revelation 21:7)

DAY 19 FRET NOT BECAUSE OF EVILDOERS

"Fret not thyself because of evildoers, neither be thou envious against the workers of iniquity. For they shall soon be cut down like the grass, and wither as the green herb". Psalm 37:1, 2

Very often we see wickedness around us, increase in workers of iniquity, and evil-doers. No doubt the prince of this world is Satan and he is making all possible endeavors to control the world systems with his wickedness. His wickedness started in the Garden of Eden when he approached the woman in a subtle way and deceived her with a cunning question and that question was "Yea, hath God said?" (Genesis 3:1) That question from the Serpent, who is the Old Dragon, the Satan, raised doubt in the mind of the woman. Satan still continues to deceive mankind with that question.

The men in Sodom were wicked and sinners before God exceedingly. (Gen 13:13).

Abram was very rich and he went out with his wife Sarai, with all the riches he had and with his brother Haram's son, Lot into the south. The riches of Abram and Lot were so great that it was hard for them to live together. There was strife between herdsmen of Abram's cattle and herdsmen of Lot's cattle. Seeing this strife Abram said to Lot to separate from him in order to prevent the strife between them. He offered to Lot that if he chose to go to the left Abram would go to the right and if he chose to go the right Abram would go to the left. Lot lifted up his eyes and saw the plain of Jordan was very pleasing to him and watered well. Therefore, Lot chose to go to the land of Jordan and lived in the cities of the plain toward Sodom. Abram dwelt in the land of Canaan. The men of Sodom were wicked and sinners before the LORD exceedingly.

The LORD blessed Abram and said to him to look toward northward, southward, eastward and westward and promised to give him and his descendants for ever the land that he saw. Abram went and lived in the plain of Mamre, which was in Hebron and he built an altar unto the LORD.

Two angels in the form of men went to Sodom one evening while Lot sat at the gate of Sodom. Lot saw them and rose up to meet them and bowed himself with his face toward the ground and requested them to stay in his house that night.

The angels refused initially but because Lot requested repeatedly they agreed to stay with him in his house. It was not long enough before that evening when men from the Sodom surrounded the house and called Lot and asked him to present the angels in men's form that they may know them.

Lot requested them not to do wickedly to them and have if they please his two virgin daughters instead. He repeated his requests not to do any wickedness to the two angels in men's form in his house. The men from Sodom pressed hard to break open the door, but the men from inside pulled Lot and smote the men outside with blindness. (Ref. Genesis Ch.19)

Lot's story goes still further but here was seen the wicked put to their shame and to suffer blindness.

DAY 20 STEPHEN SPEAKS ABOUT ABRAHAM

Many a time it occurs to believers that Abraham had faith in God from the time he was visited upon by three men (one of them was Christ himself, and two others were angels) as we read in Genesis 18th Chapter.

However, it should be noted that Abraham believed in God and had faith in Him even before the three men visited him. The God of glory appeared to Abraham. Stephen uses the phrase "our father" to make it known very clearly to the people, elders and the scribes, and the high priest that Abraham was not only their father but of him also.

We can admire the polite way Stephen addresses them by calling them as "Men, brethren, and fathers" and implores that he may be heard of his plea. The people, elders and the scribes blamed him that he spoke blasphemy against the holy place which was given to them as inheritance for being the descendants of Abraham. They also blamed him that he spoke against the Law of Moses.

Stephen says that Abraham was in Mesopotamia before he went to Charran, and there appeared to him the God of glory and asked him to "get thee out of thy country, and from thy kindred, and come into the land which I will shew thee".

Abraham did not question God as to why he was being moved out from that place and which place he was going to and how he would survive there. Abraham had faith in God that he would sustain him in all the circumstances. He believed God fully and obeyed his voice. Abraham moved out from the land of Chaldeans, in obedience to the command from God, and lived in Charran. He moved out from that place, again in obedience to the command from God and lived in Canaan.

The Scripture says that God *removed* him from one place to another and not Abraham moved out from one place to another on his own. Abraham believed God before God made covenant with him and this was even before his circumcision.

"And Abraham was ninety years old and nine, when he was circumcised in the flesh of his foreskin" (Genesis 17:24)

God blessed Abraham. His name was "Abram" when the LORD spoke to him and asked him to leave the country where he dwelt first, leave his kindred, leave his father's house and go to a land that God promised to show him.

The LORD said to him that He will make "Abram" a great nation and bless him, and make his name great, and he will be a blessing. True to the promise of God, Abraham, and his posterity are blessed.

A very serious note is to be taken here that God said that whoever curses Abraham will be cursed by God, and whoever blesses Abraham will be blessed by God. (Genesis 12:1-3).

We are warned here that even today that none of us should dare curse Abraham or his posterity through the patriarchs, the descendants of Jacob, who are the children of "Israel".

God bless the descendants of Abraham through Isaac; and also the children by faith in Lord Jesus Christ, the children of Israel, and the Nation Israel.

The knowledge shown by Stephen, of Abraham, was greater than that of the people, elders and the scribes.

DAY 21 LORD JESUS CHRIST, OUR HIGH PRIEST

"For Christ is not entered into the holy places made with hands, which are the figures of the true; but into heaven itself, now to appear in the presence of God for us: Nor yet that he should offer himself often, as the high priest entereth into the holy place every year with blood of others" (Hebrews 9:24-25)

Usually man views his present status lightly unless he compares it with his previous status from where he was elevated. He would give least importance to his present status if had forgotten the troubles and trials that he had undergone in rising up from his old status to the present status. He might think that he deserved all the blessings and they are all by his own virtue and his efforts.

Most of the Christians feel comfortable with the freedom that they have in approaching the Father through Lord Jesus Christ without realizing that God was so unapproachable in the Old Testament period.

The study of priests, high priest and the offerings and sacrifices that they had offer year after year will help Christians to appreciate the freedom they enjoy in Christ.

While the priests offered sacrifices several times a year on several occasions the high priest was authorized to enter the "Holy of Holies" only once a year to offer sin offering in a very meticulous method that God prescribed. He risked his own life while making an entry into the Holy of Holies; first with incense, second with the blood of the Lord's goat. He then confessed the sins of the people by placing his hands on live goat If the high priest made any mistake in doing these ceremonies the result would be his instant death.

"Ye also, as lively stones, are built up a spiritual house, an holy priesthood, to offer up spiritual sacrifices, acceptable to God by Jesus Christ". (1 Peter 2:5)

We have our way to the Father only through the sacrifice offered by Lord Jesus Christ on our behalf and our walk with God is by sanctification.

The sacrifices offered in the Old Testament period were the shadows of the perfect sacrifice seen in Lord Jesus Christ who died on our behalf bearing our sins upon Him in order that we may have salvation through Him. Jesus is the way, the truth and the life and no man can go the Father but by Him.

There was no way to approach God in the Old Testament period except through priests, who were mediators between God and men and through the sacrifices that they had to bring yearlong on various occasions.

The priests also had tough job to keep the fire under the altar burning always. Any error was not tolerated by God. How privileged we are that all the believers are made priests through the sacrifice of Lord Jesus Christ and He became our high priest pleading on our behalf all the time.

"Bless the LORD, O my soul: and all that is within me,

[bless] his holy name. Bless the LORD, O my soul, and forget not all his benefits: Who forgiveth all thine iniquities; who healeth all thy diseases; Who redeemeth thy life from destruction; who crowneth thee with lovingkindness and tender mercies; Who satisfieth thy mouth with good [things; so that] thy youth is renewed like the eagle's Psalm 103:1-5"

DAY 22 PEACE OFFERING

"And if his oblation be a sacrifice of peace offering, if he offer it of the herd; whether it be a male or female, he shall offer it without blemish before the LORD" (Leviticus 3:1)

There is a very sublime concept involved in the peace offering and as title indicates the man offering peace offering seeks peace with God. It shows the desire to have fellowship with God. Indeed, God responds by offering fellowship with man.

Loving as He is, God always cherished fellowship with man and desired to commune with him. With Adam and Eve falling into sin they lost fellowship with God and consequently we all have inherited that sin from him. God provided way to go near him and have fellowship with Him provided our sins are put away from us and righteousness is imputed to us.

The imputation is righteousness to man is possible only at the discretion of God when all the conditions that He prescribed are fulfilled. These conditions were in different form in the Old Testament period than that of New Testament period.

We would not have realized the benefits we have in Jesus Christ unless we knew the pattern of worship that was laid out for man in the Old Testament. Every bit of worship of the Old Testament was shadow that was fulfilled in the New Testament. It is therefore, essential that we should not discard reading and understanding Old Testament. There is no way for man to get rid of his sin unless the prescribed sacrifice is offered to God and its blood is shed.

We part take of his provision and God participates in our gratitude. The peace offering is eaten by the priests, the children of priests and the family of the one who offers it indicating that there is peace established among all of them. (Leviticus 7:28-34, Numbers 18:9-11, Deuteronomy 7:7-8, 17-18).

God says that if the peace offering is from the herd, then irrespective of the gender of the offering it should be without any blemish and if his is from the flock, then the lamb, irrespective of male or female should be without blemish.

If he offers a lamb for his offering, then he shall offer it before the LORD. This reminds us also of the peace that was going to unite Jews and Gentiles into one body of Christ, the Church.

Man should offer his peace offering at the door of the tabernacle of the congregation by laying his hands on it signifying that he is transferring all his sins on to that offering, and kill it.

Aaron and his sons, who are priests, shall sprinkle the blood upon the altar round about. The peace offering should be made by fire unto the LORD.

The internal organs and the entire fat that connects them, both the kidneys with the fat on them near the loins, and the long lobe of liver should be burnt on top of the burnt offering that which is placed on the burning wood by the priests on behalf of the one who offers them as peace offering. It is a food offering and the aroma of it is pleasing to the LORD. The burnt offering is made to indicate that the man offering is agreeing to be consecrated fully to the LORD, and the peace offering thereon indicates the willingness to serve the LORD.

LORD Jesus Christ broke down the middle wall of partition between Jews and Gentiles after having abolished in his flesh the enmity, even the law of commandments contained in ordinances to make the two into "one new man" by making peace between the two (Ephesians 2:14-15).

He made peace through the blood that he shed for us on the cross in order to reconcile unto him all things in earth and in heaven (Colossians 1:20).

We, who are born again, are justified by faith have peace with God through our Lord Jesus Christ, who was our propitiation and substitute (Romans 3:24-26 and Romans 5:1)

The Law was given by Moses, but grace and truth came by Jesus Christ (John 1:17, John 1:29).

There is only one way for salvation. Jesus is the way, the truth and the life. (John 14:6). Speaking to Nicodemus Jesus said

"…Verily, verily, I say unto thee, Except a man be born again, he cannot see the kingdom of God" (John 3:3).

DAY 23 GOSPEL TO GENTILES

Granting salvation to the Gentiles was in the plan of God from before the foundation of the world. Apostle Paul was sent to be a minister of Gospel of Jesus Christ to the Gentiles, Peter spoke of salvation to the Gentiles, and Stephen also spoke of the salvation to the Gentiles.

However, we should not forget the fact that the promises, adoption, the glory, covenants, giving of the law, and the service of God belonged to the Israelites.

For if thou wert cut out of the olive tree which is wild by nature, and wert graffed contrary to nature into a good olive tree: how much more shall these, which be the natural branches, be graffed into their own olive tree? (Romans 11:24)

The people, elders and the scribes took pride in saying that they are the children of Abraham, and their holy place is Jerusalem. Their castigation of Stephen was on the count that he spoke blasphemy against Abraham, Jerusalem, and the Law of Moses.

Defending his stand Stephen points to the fact that he was the descendant of Abraham, and Holy Place Jerusalem is as holy to him as it was to them. He pleads that he did not speak a word against the Law of Moses or the Holy place, but he spoke of what was in the will of God. Stephen's point in his defense was that even if he had spoken something against them or the Law of Moses, he was not at fault, because it was not the Holy place or the Law of

Moses that gave salvation to anybody. He was emphasizing on the point that they do not need to be proud of their lineage from Abraham.

In order to curtail their pride that they showed in their lineage from that of Abraham, Stephen speaks about "Abraham", who was "Abram" before he was blessed and that he came out from the land of Ur of Chaldees.

It was God who brought him out of the land of Chaldees, where people worshipped idols, and other gods. God moved "Abram" out of these people and out of that land of Gentiles and gave him the land of Canaan.

Stephen quotes history from the Old Testament and says that Terah took his son, "Abram", and "Lot" the son of "Haram" and "Sarai", "Abram"'s wife and moved out from the land of Ur of Chaldees and went first upto Haraan and dwelt there. (Now these are the generations of Terah: Terah begat Abram, Nahor, and Haran; and Haran begat Lot. (Genesis 11:27))

Later they came out from Haraan and went to dwell in Canaan. There is, therefore, no reason, says Stephen, to be proud of calling themselves as the descendants of Abraham.

[References:(Genesis 11:31, Genesis 12:1, Joshua 24:2, Nehemiah 9:7, Isaiah 41:2, Isaiah 51:1)]

DAY 24 THE ONLY SAVIOR

"And he said, Take heed that ye be not deceived: for many shall come in my name, saying, I am Christ; and the time draweth near: go ye not therefore after them" (Luke 21:8)

It is usual among people to hurl their indignation on incurring huge expenditure on functions to honor distinguished guests.

While it is true that expenditure is inevitable for honoring distinguishing guests the indignation hurled at them would more often than not is not worth the anger. The reason why such anger is expressed usually is because they do not fully understand the purpose.

The creator of this universe, Lord Jesus Christ, who is the Almighty, walked on the earth just as any human would. He was in the form of a servant in the likeness of man to show to the mankind the right way to salvation and eternal bliss.

The disciples of Jesus were indignant on the huge expenditure incurred on an alabaster box containing very precious ointment of spikenard being opened and the contents being poured by the woman on the feet of Lord Jesus Christ. The woman bought the ointment at very high price and brought it to the feet of the Lord and worshipped Him.

The Jews did not accept Lord Jesus Christ as their Messiah. It was two days after the feast of the Passover and unleavened bread that the chief priests and the scribes conspired to take hold of Lord Jesus Christ by their crafty intentions and put Him to death.

However, they feared to lay hands on Lord Jesus Christ because it was feast day. The people in Bethany in the house of Simon the leper would have caused surely a great uproar if such an attempt was made to lay hold on the savior of the world, Lord Jesus Christ, who sat for a meal there.

"And there were some that had indignation within themselves, and said, Why was this waste of the ointment made? For it might have been sold for more than three hundred pence, and have been given to the poor. And they murmured against her" (Mark 14:4-5)

The Lord knew their indignation and heard their murmurings and said to them to let the woman be free from accusations. He questioned them as to why they were troubling her. He said to them that the poor are there always with them but He would be there with them always. He took note of the good work of the woman and her worship.

The Lord attested that her good work to worship Him will be remembered for ever wherever the Gospel is preached. Her action signified the oncoming death, burial and resurrection of Lord Jesus Christ shortly after the Passover festival.

"She hath done what she could: she is come aforehand to anoint my body to the burying" (Mark 14:8)

Accept Lord Jesus Christ as your personal Savior. The LORD Says:

"Look unto me, and be ye saved, all the ends of the earth: for I am God, and there is none else" (Isaiah 45:22)

DAY 25 SANCTIFICATION BY THE WORD

"That he might sanctify and cleanse it with the washing of water by the word" (Ephesians 5:26)

Queen Esther was chosen by King Ahasuerus to be his queen not before she underwent cleansing process for a total period of twelve months; six months with oil of myrrh and six months with sweet odors.

It was after queen Vashti banned to appear before the King anymore because she refused to present herself at the feast hosted by the King and to show her beauty before the princes from Persia and Media, the nobles and princes of the provinces and servants who gathered at the feast hosted by him in his third year of reign.

King Ahasuerus ruled from India even unto Ethiopia over one hundred seven and twenty provinces. (Ref. Esther 1:1)

When Queen Vashti, who was very beautiful, refused to present herself in the presence of the King and to show her beauty before the dignitaries the king banned her at the behest of Memucan who was one of the seven wise princes of Persia and Media.

King Ahasuerus said that fair young women be sent to him turn by turn to please him and if the king was pleased she would be his queen or else she would be his concubine. It was a great challenge for Esther to take up the risky task and accepted for cleansing as specified. She successfully passed the test from the King and became his queen. Esther was the daughter of Mordecai's uncle. Mordecai was a Jew carried away as captive from Jerusalem and they both became very useful instruments in the hands of God to fulfill His desire to redeem the Jews.

This picture was indirectly referred to when Apostle Paul wrote about the Church that needs sanctification with the washing of water by the word. The husband desires that his wife be pure before he married her.

The cleansing of Esther was an allusion to the cleansing of the Church. Paul writes that wives and husbands need to submit one to another in the fear or the Lord; wives to their husbands just as unto the Lord because husband is the head of the wife even as Christ is the head of the Church. Husbands are instructed to love their wives just as Christ also loved the Church and gave Himself for it.

Lord Jesus Christ is the savior and Church is the body and bride of Christ. He is the head of the Church and the Church is His body and each believer is a member of the said body.

Lord Jesus gave His life unto the Church and He keeps sanctifying it and cleansing it with washing of water by the word in order that He may present unto Himself the Church as a glorious bride, without any wrinkle or any spot but as holy and without any blemish.

The sanctification was seen in the Old Testament period when Aaron and his sons washed their hands and their feet. It was the commandment of the LORD who spoke through

Moses saying that he should make a "Laver" of brass and make its foot also of brass and fill it with water and place it between the tabernacle of the congregation and the altar. The high priest and the priests were commanded that when they enter the tabernacle of the congregation they shall wash with water and if they violated God's commandment they died instantly (Ref. Exodus Ch. 30:17-21)

"Now ye are clean through the word which I have spoken unto you" (John 15:3)

"Jesus answered, Verily, verily, I say unto thee, Except a man be born of water and of the Spirit, he cannot enter into the kingdom of God". (John 3:5)/div>";

DAY 26 JOSEPH'S ACKNOWLEDGMENT

"And his brothers also went and fell down before his face; and they said, Behold, we are your servants. And Joseph said unto them, Fear not: for am I in the place of God? But as for you, you thought evil against me; but God meant it unto good, to bring to pass, as it is this day, to save many people alive". (Genesis 50:18-20)

Joseph's brothers did not like the interpretations Joseph gave of the dreams he dreamt. Joseph's father rebuked him when he interpreted his second dream.

Joseph's brothers felt jealous of Joseph and conspired to do harm to Joseph.

"And they said one to another, Behold, this dreamer comes. Come now therefore, and let us slay him, and cast him into some pit, and we will say, Some evil beast has devoured him: and we shall see what will become of his dreams". (Genesis 37:19-20)

Joseph's brothers cast Joseph in a waterless pit. Later he was pulled out by Midianites who sold him to Ishmaelites, who in turn, sold him to the Egyptians. Joseph proved himself worthy of his calling by escaping from the seduction of Potiphar's wife.

Joseph remained true and honest to master, Potiphar. Things did not seem to be going in favor of Joseph, when he was trying to escape from the trouble. He actually got in to the trouble when Potiphar's wife accused him of molesting her. Joseph's master gave credence to his wife and sent Joseph in to prison.

Later, when Joseph interpreted Pharaoh's dreams he was released from the prison and Pharaoh made him governor in the land of Egypt. He had great authority in Egypt.

"And Pharaoh said unto Joseph, Since God has showed you all this, there is none so discreet and wise as you are: You shall be over my house, and according unto your word shall all my people be ruled: only in the throne will I be greater than you". (Genesis 41:39-40)

"And Pharaoh said unto Joseph, I am Pharaoh, and without you shall no man lift up his hand or foot in all the land of Egypt". (Genesis 41:44)

In spite of having all the authority on his side, Joseph acknowledged in Chapter 45:8 "So then, it was not you who sent me here, but god. He made me father to Pharaoh, lord of his entire household and ruler of all Egypt."

Let us turn to Luke Chapter 23 verse 34 Jesus said, "Father forgive them, for they do not know what they are doing…"

How great is the love of Jesus Christ, the Savior of this world. While chief priests and the teachers of the law, who were standing near the cross of Calvary, accusing the Son of God, Jesus Christ, While Herod and his soldiers were ridiculing him and mocked him, Oh! Then, Jesus said," Father forgive them, for they do not know what they are doing…"

The people there were representatives of all of us. We were all crucifying Jesus on the cross of Calvary. We all nailed his palms to the hard cross, and crowned him with crown of thorns

Should we not receive him as our savior and acknowledge him as our Lord? Yes, Jesus is the Lord. He is the savior. Let us worship him in spirit and truth.

DAY 27 THE WORD SHALL NOT RETURN VOID

"So shall my word be that goeth forth out of my mouth: it shall not return unto me void, but it shall accomplish that which I please, and it shall prosper in the thing whereto I sent it "(Isaiah 55:11)

There was a king by name Macedon who renovated and beautified the city and it became a Roman Colony. It was most remarkable city because many battles took place around this city.

The battles include one was that of Julius Caesar and Pompey the great, and another one was that of Cassius and Brutus. "Philippi" was a chief city in Macedonia. However, for Christians this city was important one because it was a city where Apostle Paul established a Church in a very small way in the house of a woman named "Lydia", yet it grew to very important known Church. God's word will not go waste but it will achieve its purpose for which it was sent.

The woman named Lydia was a seller of purple from the city of Thyatira. Paul spoke to her about God and she readily received the Lord Jesus Christ as her savior. Lydia and her household were baptized and she constrained Paul to stay with them. Thus a small church was established in Lydia's house at Philippi.

The beginning of the Church was very small. Lydia and Philippian Jailor were among those who converted there.

The start was small but the end was very good. Paul was not discouraged with small start. Philippi was a city where the Jailor was also saved. Paul worked very hard for the Church at Philippi and writes:

"For to me to live is Christ, and to die is gain". (Philippians 1:21)

As Paul and his co-workers were boldly proclaiming the Gospel, once a girl possessed with evil spirit met them, and cried out loudly saying repeatedly for many days "These men are the servants of the most high God, which shew unto us the way of salvation".

Paul was grieved and commanded the evil spirit to get out of her in the name of Jesus Christ. The evil spirit left the girl immediately. In the meanwhile, the masters of the girl perceived that they lost their earnings earned from her soothsaying. The masters lay false charges against Paul and his co-workers that they preached against their customs and presented them before the Roman authorities.

The magistrates rent off their clothes and commanded them to be beaten and cast into prison. Paul and Silas did not get discouraged even while they were in prison but they sang songs, which were heard by the other prisoners. God answered their songs and prayers by bringing in huge earthquake that shook the foundations of the prison and the doors were opened and everyone's bands were loosed.

The Jailor was afraid and thought that the prisons escaped. He thought that he would be cast into prison and drew his sword to commit suicide. Then, Paul cried out loudly and said to him "do thyself no harm: for we are all here". The gesture moved the heart of the Jailor who asked Paul as to what he should do to get saved. Paul and his co-workers said to him to believe on the Lord Jesus Christ and if he did so not only he would be saved but his whole house would be saved. They spoke to him and everyone in his house more about Jesus. The Jailor believed on Jesus Christ.

"And he took them the same hour of the night, and washed their stripes; and was baptized, he and all his, straightway. And when he had brought them into his house, he set meat before them, and rejoiced, believing in God with all his house" (Acts 16:33-34)

The magistrates sent the sergeants and commanded Paul and his co-workers be allowed to be gone where they wished to go but Paul took objection that they were held as prisoners and were asked to leave in secret without any tenable reason and, therefore, he sought that the magistrates and sergeants go to the prison and fetch them out openly declaring them innocent. The magistrates and sergeants went and brought them out and requested them to leave the city. Paul and his co-workers left prison and went to Lydia's house where brethren comforted them and they departed from the city. (Ref: Acts 16:25-40)

DAY 28 WORSHIP GOD
IN SPIRIT AND IN TRUTH

Worship is the reverence paid to God. As believers in Lord Jesus Christ, we worship the Father through His Son, Lord Jesus Christ, according to the New Testament pattern, where Jesus takes the prominence in our worship.

Jesus said, in John 10:17 "Therefore doth my Father love me, because I lay down my life, that I might take it again".

In John 10:30 he said "I and my Father are one"

Jesus said in John 4:23 "But the hour cometh, and now is, when the true worshippers shall worship the Father in spirit and in truth: for the Father seeketh such to worship him".

It is obvious here that the true worshippers will worship the Father in spirit and in truth and as the "Father" in heaven and Jesus are one the worship that we render to Jesus is acceptable to the Father in heaven. Here, it becomes necessary for us to know what exactly "worship" is. Worship according to New Testament pattern is not fleshly nor is it physical. God is Sprit, therefore, our worship should be in spirit and in truth and not physical nor should be fleshly (John 4:24). We see in Old Testament the pattern of worship had in it, a physical structure called, Tabernacle, Priests with special clothing, Lamp stands, burning of incense, usage of musical instruments, and sacrifice of animals. These all give us physical and fleshly senses.

New Testament pattern of worship is based on Hebrews

9:11-12, where Jesus is seen as the high priest and perfect tabernacle, not made with the hands of men, or with the blood of goats, or calves, but with his own blood, which he shed for us at the cross of Calvary, and obtained eternal redemption for us.

We are no more strangers and foreigners but fellow citizens with the saints. Jesus Christ is the corner stone and in him we are built together for a habitation of God through the Spirit. (Ref. Ephesians 2:19-22)

New Testament pattern of worship is centered on Jesus Christ, and spiritual aspects of life. The believers in Christ are one household of God and are built on the foundation laid by the Apostles and Prophets. Lord Jesus Christ himself is the corner stone of such building. All those saved in the precious blood of Jesus are fitly framed together and grow in the grace of God and are parts of that holy temple of the Lord. We are built together for habitation of God through the Sprit

Every born again child of God may worship God in spirit and in truth. Let us bow down to him and acknowledge him as our Lord and Savior. Let us sing songs and hymns of worship. Such worship rendered by the child of God is acceptable unto him. The observance of "Lord's Supper" by breaking bread and drinking from the cup is a great way of worshiping Lord Jesus Christ. We remember the death of Jesus Christ, his burial and resurrection and his ascension.

"And when he had given thanks, he brake it, and said, Take, eat: this is my body, which is broken for you: this do in remembrance of me. After the same manner also he took the cup, when he had supped, saying, This cup is the new testament in my blood: this do ye, as oft as ye drink it, in remembrance of me". (1 Corinthians 11:24-25)

DAY 29 AS FAR EAST IS FROM THE WEST

"As far as the east is from the west, so far hath he removed our transgressions from us" (Psalms 103:12)

It is interesting to note that the Number forty signifies testing period in Scriptures. Jonah preached saying:

"And Jonah began to enter into the city a day's journey, and he cried, and said, Yet forty days, and Nineveh shall be overthrown" (Jonah 3:4)

The significance of this number, 'forty' was great inasmuch as in the life of Jesus, who lived on this earth only for thirty and half years, spread the message of repentance and the "kingdom of God that was at hand" for three and half years. Before starting his ministry upon this earth, Jesus fasted for forty nights and forty days in the wilderness. It was forty days and forty nights that there was rain during Noah's period.

Moses spent forty years in Pharaoh's house as a child and young man, and fled to Midian after killing an Egyptian, who was ill-treating one of his kinsmen and there he lived for forty years in that strange life with his wife, and looking after his father-in-law Jethro's sheep and had two children there. After that he rose up as a leader of Israel with a call from none other than God himself, and led Israelites for forty years and sadly he himself could not enter Canaan, the Promised Land because of his small disobedience.

While the life of Moses ended before seeing the promised land of Canaan, the death of Lord Jesus Christ was a glorious one upon the cross of Calvary for the remission of sins of man. Jesus was humiliated by his own men, who crucified him for no fault after beating up in unimaginable ways. Jesus bore all the suffering for the sake of saving you and me from the sins and to give eternal life for us. The salvation is at hand to any person who confesses sins and accepts Jesus Christ as his/her personal savior and say by mouth that he is the Lord.

The message of the Gospel is very simple and it is, "For God so loved the world, that he gave his only begotten Son, that whosoever believeth in him should not perish, but have everlasting life" John 3:16 When there is no hope we will find hope in Jesus Christ who promised eternal life if we confess our sins to him. God says in

Psalms 103:12

"As far as the east is from the west, so far hath he removed our transgressions from us".

It is true. Once we confess us sins to God and accept Jesus Christ as our personal savior we are saved. I have heard this message when I was young boy and I am happy that I confessed my sins to God and accepted Jesus Christ as my personal Savior.

We do not know how far East is from the West but we know that they are opposite poles. It gives happiness to us that our sins are removed from me as far as East is from the West and God never sees them again. Jesus said, he will never remember our sins after cleansing us from the unrighteousness. He gives us his righteousness to us and when a sinner is saved there is joy in heaven in the presence of angels.

DAY 30 REDEEMED BY THE PRECIOUS BLOOD

"Forasmuch as ye know that ye were not redeemed with corruptible things, as silver and gold, from your vain conversation received by tradition from your fathers; But with the precious blood of Christ, as of a lamb without blemish and without spot" (1 Peter 1:18-19)

Moses had three major roles to perform:

1. to be the leader of the children of Israel
2. to hand over the Law as given by God to the children of Israel and
3. to mediate between the children of Israel and God.

Lord Jesus Christ came into this world as THE WAY, THE TRUTH, and THE LIFE

1. to redeem man from his sin
2. to give man the beatitudes as found in Matthew Chapter 5, 6 and 7 and
3. to mediate between man and the Father.

Jesus gave two great commandments as found in Mark 12:30-31

"And thou shalt love the Lord thy God with all thy heart, and with all thy soul, and with all thy mind, and with all thy strength: this is the first commandment. And the second is like, namely this, Thou shalt love thy neighbour as thyself.

There is none other commandment greater than these",

The two commandments given by Lord Jesus contain the essence of all the Ten Commandments, and He is our mediator between us and the Father.

Moses was the deliverer of God's children physically, while Jesus was the deliverer spiritually of His people Jews first and the Gentiles next.

"But now hath he obtained a more excellent ministry, by how much also he is the mediator of a better covenant, which was established upon better promises" Hebrews 8:6

The New Testament covenant is the best of all that we could receive from Jesus. The Old covenant included in it the shadows and types of the things to come and the New Testament contains the anti-types and the substance. Old Testament law was stringent in nature, which demanded unconditional obedience to the Law whereas the New Testament demands sincere obedience, repentance of sins to Jesus and accepting Him as the Lord. We are saved by grace through faith.

During the Old Testament period sins were not fully forgiven but they were covered when the sacrifices were offered. In Jesus, who was without any sin and without any blemish, and who became sin for us on the cross, are sins fully forgiven of all the Old Testament saints and of those in New Testament Period.

DAY 31 YE ARE THE CHILDREN OF LIGHT

"But ye, brethren, are not in darkness, that that day should overtake you as a thief. Ye are all the children of light, and the children of the day: we are not of the night, nor of darkness". (1 Thessalonians 5:4-5)

Speaking about his coming again Jesus said that we who are in the light need not worry about it. We who are the children of light will gladly say "Amen. Even so, come, Lord Jesus". It is joy to be caught up to meet the Lord in the air and thereafter to be with the Lord for ever and ever.

The second coming of Jesus is terror for those who have not accepted Jesus as their personal savior. It is terror for them because they are the children of darkness. As for us we are saved and are in the light. We are called as "the children of light".

The times and seasons are given for us to follow but not to predict the date of his coming again. The time and day of coming again of Jesus is not revealed to anyone. It is known only to the Father.

After the expiry of the Great Tribulation Period when the Lord steps on the Mount of Olives, every eye shall see him. Everyone who pierced the Lord and every one on the earth will cry for him because he comes to rule. He will not be coming like a lamb again, but he will come like a lion to rule the earth and to rule every nation.

Every tongue shall confess then that Jesus is the Lord. Their eyes will be opened to acknowledge that he was the Messiah who was to come and who came for the lost sheep of Israel once. (Matthew 15:24, 1 Thessalonians 4:16, 17 and Revelation 1:7)

It was with great agony and suffering that our Lord Jesus walked from Gethsemane to Golgotha bearing cross on his shoulder. We were under the bondage of sin and were supposed to carry that cross but Jesus carried that cross on our behalf. Had not Jesus suffered and died on behalf of us we would not have received salvation.

It pleased the Father to bruise Jesus. Even though Jesus knew how hard it was to carry our cross and our sin, he submitted to the will of the Father and said "thy will be done".

"He went away again the second time, and prayed, saying, O my Father, if this cup may not pass away from me, except I drink it, thy will be done". (Matthew 26:42)

On either side of Jesus two thieves were crucified and that was done to humiliate Jesus that he was equal with them. Large nails were run through his palms and feet on to the cross.

Entire blood from his body was shed and every drop of the blood shed was for cleansing our sins. A crown of thorns was platted on his head; people spat on His face and pierced Him.

"And when they had platted a crown of thorns, they put it upon his head, and a reed in his right hand: and they bowed the knee before him, and mocked him, saying, Hail, King of the Jews!" (Matthew 27:29)

He was mocked as King of kings; indeed He was the King of kings, but the way they treated Him was unbearable. Jesus Christ is the Son of God and he is the second person in Trinity. He became man for our sake and came into this world to die for our sake, so that we may receive salvation. Death could not hold Jesus in the grave. He was triumphant over death and rose from the dead.

Later he ascended in to heaven and now seated on the right hand of the Majesty. He is the living God. We are the children of light and we do not have fellowship with the works of darkness.

"And have no fellowship with the unfruitful works of darkness, but rather reprove them." (Ephesians 5:11)

www.ingramcontent.com/pod-product-compliance
Lightning Source LLC
Chambersburg PA
CBHW060037040426
42331CB00032B/991